INSURANCE AND
REINSURANCE RUN-OFF

British Library Cataloguing in Publication Data
Wedge, Peter
Insurance and Reinsurance Run-off
1st Ed.
1. Insurance
1. Title

ISBN 1 85609 211 9

Swiss Re New Markets

This publication is sponsored by Swiss Re New Markets.

The views expressed by the author are personal ones and do not reflect the views of Swiss Re New Markets.

INSURANCE AND REINSURANCE RUN-OFF

by

Peter Wedge

LONDON
WITHERBY & CO LTD
32–36 Aylesbury Street
London EC1R 0ET

Published 2001

WITHERBY

PUBLISHERS

ISBN 1 85609 211 9

Printed and Published by
WITHERBY & CO. LTD
32-36 Aylesbury Street, London EC1R 0ET
Tel No. 020 7251 5341 Fax No. 020 7251 1296
International Tel No. +44 20 7251 5341
International Fax No. +44 20 7251 1296
E-mail: books@witherbys.co.uk
www: witherbys.com

PREFACE

Subject

The book is concerned with the strategy adopted by an insurance/reinsurance company once a decision to discontinue writing business has been taken. One of the options is to enter into formal run-off. However, run-off is only one method of several possible methods of ending/transferring the liability, although it is easily the most common, perhaps taking place in 90% of all cases. We will examine the best ways that a company can formulate a discontinued business strategy and also explain the process of an Insurer/Reinsurer

- entering into run-off;
- being in run-off; and
- exiting run-off.

Focus of the book and its intended use

This book concentrates principally upon

- the UK experience in general[i], as opposed to the American or European. Inasmuch as the phenomenon of and dynamics of run-off are similar in the USA or Europe (depending upon the precise regulatory framework under which the Reinsurer is operating) the basic principles can be applied to these other countries. One significant difference, however, between the UK and the USA is the legal process of liquidation, and this has a large impact upon the operation of insolvent companies;
- general insurance business rather than life insurance;
- English law;
- English market practice.

This book is therefore targeted mainly at executives in

- reinsurance companies;
- reinsurance companies in run-off;

(i) It is worth noting that entities writing business in the London market are subject to unique procedures and influences. A major difference in dealing with a London Market entity is that it will usually participate on a policy as part of a subscription market. It will take only a share of each policy and will be on risk with numerous co-insuring companies and/or syndicates.

- reinsurance companies or specialised funds interested in acquiring discontinued lines of business;
- run-off management companies;
- financial institutions teams in investment banks;
- lawyers specialising in reinsurance;
- accountants specialising in reinsurance;
- brokers;
- reinsurance consultants.

As such, it must necessarily cover a wide spectrum of knowledge and experience of run-off. For this reason, the aim is to lay down the general principles in a wide number of areas leaving the specifics to be gathered from more specialised texts (if available). The aim is to provide a 'hands-on' approach to a complicated and, at times, technical subject. In short, it is seeking to demystify run-off, enabling the reader to understand current themes and trends and to suggest a sensible and practical way to deal with the problems of run-off.

It should be noted that the book contains insurance and reinsurance jargon, although this is explained and defined wherever possible.

Much more could have been written on most subjects but the goal has been to keep the book within manageable proportions. Therefore, some subjects have been deliberately omitted: for example, readers will have to look elsewhere for the application of information technology to the administration of companies in run-off.[ii]

It is possible that the book will be expanded in future editions – comments and suggestions regarding any omissions or areas of interest are welcome. This book may be seen as a stepping stone for the academic study of this subject. Unfortunately, it is feasible that new developments have occurred during the preparation of this book – some of which have not been covered.

Thanks to all of those in the London market who assisted, officially and unofficially, in the preparation of this book. Special thanks to Patricia Perelli, Ashley K. Dhadialla, Gregory Hopp, and Christian Wells.

Peter Wedge, Zurich 2001

(ii) With the growing importance of e-commerce and the Internet in general, this subject may come to dominate the run-off industry in the future. For more on this subject generally refer to P.Wedge – Chartered Insurance Institute Textbook – *"Claims Management"* May 2000 and A.Starrs – *"How insurance has arrived at the real point of virtualisation"* – Insurance Day, March 9 2000.

ABOUT THE AUTHOR

Peter Wedge BSc (Econ); FCII; PG Dip.Law, Chartered Insurer is an Associate Director in the Legal & Claims Department at Swiss Re New Markets, Zurich. He is Technical Editor of the CII Textbook "The Application of Reinsurance", is the main author of the CII Textbook "Claims Management", and is also Editor of two manuals published by the Association of Run-off Companies regarding commutations and inspections of records. He has held a part-time post as Lecturer in Reinsurance at the London Guildhall University. Having studied risk management and insurance at Nottingham University as part of his first degree, he initially worked for five years in the reinsurance broking industry followed by seven years as a Senior Consultant for Chiltington. He specialized in the handling of latent claims, inspections of records, portfolio analysis, and commutation strategy. He has carried out assignments in the USA, France, Germany, Denmark, Sweden, and the UK having spent four years in Germany. Following this, he spent one year as a Team Leader in the commutations department of Equitas. In 1999 he returned to full-time education obtaining a legal qualification at university in Oxford.

Contact Details: peter_wedge@swissre.com
Telephone: +41 1285 6379

CONTENTS

Diagram 1 – Stages of a reinsurance company's life from establishment to dissolution

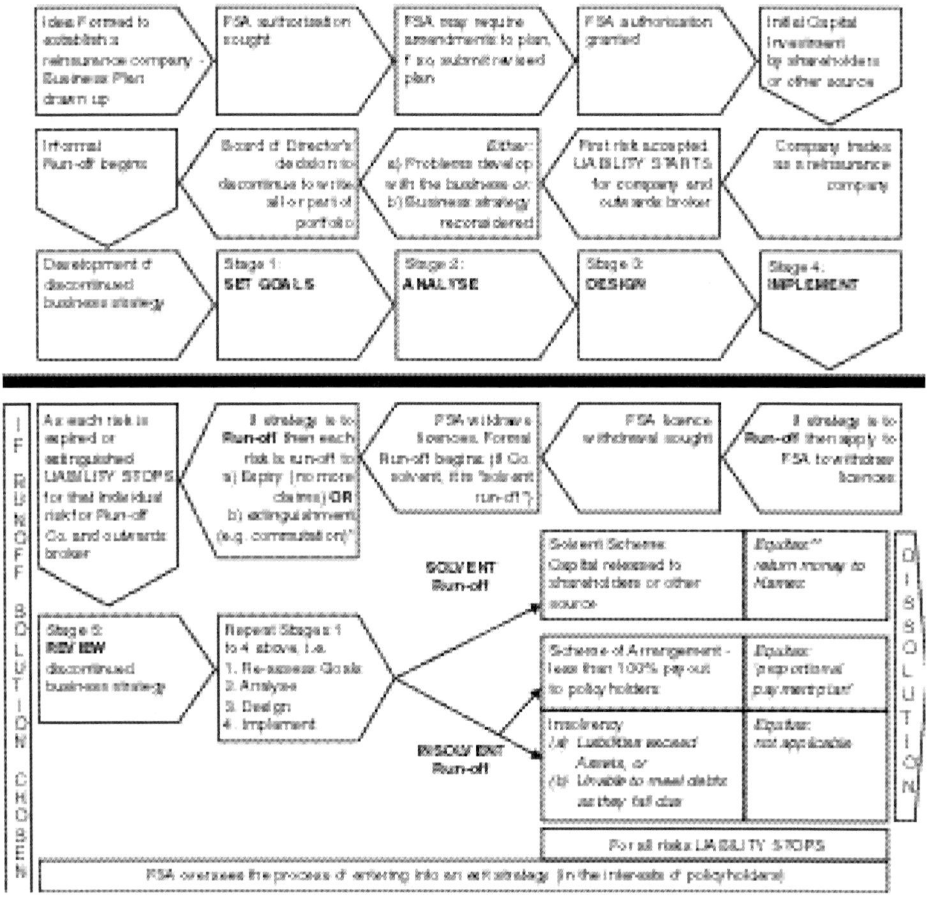

This diagram shows one possible sequence of events from the time that a reinsurance company is established until it is dissolved. Following the decision to discontinue writing new business has been taken, the company must develop its discontinued business strategy. One of the strategies it is to enter into formal run-off (*shown by the area below the black line*). However, run-off is only one method of several possible methods of ending/transferring the liability, although it is easily the most common, perhaps taking place in 90% of all cases. Other options are discussed later in the book. The FSA has an important supervisory role in this process (with the interests of the policyholders at its heart).

**Expiry of a risk issued on a loss-occurring basis takes place when there is no longer any liability under the contract. In practical terms, this is when a long period has elapsed since the last claim has been advised. In legal terms liability may continue. Therefore, to ensure legal liability is at an end, the risk should be extinguished by agreement (e.g. commutation) **Equitas – see later in this book.*

CHAPTER 1: INTRODUCTION

The fundamental problem of run-off is one of finite assets versus uncertain liabilities. However, on the assumption that ultimate losses have been correctly assessed, the development of an effective strategy for discontinued business can avoid insolvency.

1.1 Introduction

The aim of this book is to consider the process of run-off and its associated problems and to review both new and existing solutions.

More specifically, we are looking to explain:

(a) The **role of run-off**[i] within the context of discontinued business[ii] as a whole.

(b) The **different agendas** of the diverse groups[iii] (referred to as stakeholders) interested in the outcome of a run-off

(c) The advantages of utilising a **formalised approach** to the problems of run-off[iv] at the three key stages:

- entering run-off
- the run-off period itself
- exiting run-off

(d) **Alternatives** to run-off

The administrative burden and the cost of extinguishing liabilities to

---

(i) In very simple terms, Run-off is that stage of an insurance/reinsurance entity's life after it has closed its doors to new and renewal business. In the insurance/reinsurance industry the liabilities arising out of policies written have to be administered and claims paid. In essence, the insurance/reinsurance company becomes a claims-paying machine. A more precise definition is provided below.

(ii) Discontinued business in this context means a class or type of business which is no longer written. The interrelationship between discontinued business and run-off is explained below.

(iii) The different groups are referred to as stakeholders – each group has a stake in the outcome, but their needs and interests may well conflict. The basic stakeholders are regulators, policy holders, shareholders, employees, contract workers, management, brokers etc. and this topic is discussed further below.

(iv) In particular the development of a strategy to cope with the problems is set out and explained. In adopting a formalised approach to the development of a strategy for discontinued business, one can ensure that no major omissions are made. That is to say no significant issues are overlooked which may have an adverse impact upon the strategy ultimately adopted.

finality is huge, and is rarely budgeted for adequately. With an increase in the trend for Insurers and Reinsurers to go into run-off or become insolvent it is critical that insurance/reinsurance companies are well equipped to deal with this eventuality. Currently, there is often a lack of appropriate strategy to deal with the consequences of run-off and to appreciate and develop the myriad of skills required (be it technical, actuarial or managerial). Therefore, the run-off period is often too long and frequently results in an unsatisfactory outcome for all parties concerned – insolvency. There is both a great need and reward for developing a formalised strategy to deal effectively with the problem of run-off. With an appropriate strategy in place the Insurer/Reinsurer in run-off can face the future with greater certainty and a defined plan. He can take steps to realise specific goals, which often relate to the return of capital to the shareholders, rather than dissipating all the assets in the administration of the run-off itself. In short, control is retained and business efficiency is regained.

At present the history of companies in run-off in the UK is not very encouraging – virtually all companies which go into run-off whilst solvent become insolvent.

A short description of run-off

Run-off is the period when the insurance/reinsurance company still has to pay claims under old policies but does not issue new (or renewal) policies for that type of business anymore. These claims are paid out of the pot of money the company already has accumulated from premiums and investment income (and certain parts of these claims may be recoverable from reinsurance protections). If the company does not have enough money available at the right time, or has insufficient money, the company is insolvent. There are three central objectives, which any run-off entity must deal with:

- reduce administration costs;
- centralise credit control, that is, identify all recoveries due from one party (known as "principal to principal accounting");
- commute pro-actively, that is, enter into agreements which bring the liabilities to an end in return for a cash payment now.

In order to achieve each of these central aims there are a large number of activities and processes which must be put in place. The core activities consist of commuting, valuing assets and liabilities, managing the inwards claims and reinsurance processes, and investing. Companies in run-off have a much greater emphasis on cashflow than a company actively writing insurance business. This is because, other than the cash generated from its reinsurance claims and investments (and to a very limited extent from return premiums and commissions) there is no alternative revenue stream and, unless the entity in run-off is part of a group of companies, often no access to additional capital. Because in run-off the revenue stream is uncertain, there is a greater need to optimise business efficiency.

The *main players* in the run-off industry are as follows:

Financial Rating Agency – A monitor and analyst. Assesses a company's ability to pay claims and their general financial security. They have less interest in companies actually in run-off, since their fees come from live companies.

Investment Banker – A professional advisor. Advises buyers on purchases of companies and alternative discontinued business strategies. Expert in strategies and the workings of the capital markets. Dynamic and highly professional, but can be expensive.

Run-off buyer – An optimist. Often looking to buy a portfolio of companies in run-off and weld them together. A rare breed, but specialists in their field. Can see value embedded in a portfolio of business which appears to others as if it is full of liabilities and problems. Relishes a challenge. Occasionally the acquired portfolio gets the better of them, but in many instances their formalised no-nonsense business methods manage to turn the portfolio round and they are able to take out the remaining capital out of the company and earn substantial consultancy fees for their subsidiary companies along the way. Has a strong ability to see the woods from the trees.

Lawyer – Professional advisor and hand-holder who sets out the legal parameters of any plan and litigates claims etc. when disputes arise[v]. Can advise on legal compliance including setting up Schemes of Arrangement and the intricacies of insolvency procedures. More specific services relate to the legal aspects of inspections of records; commutation agreements (i.e. an agreement to release the Reinsurer

(v) In the last several years, there has been an ongoing, explosive increase in the number and magnitude of disputes arising from reinsurance agreements. In the past, reinsurance agreements have received little judicial attention, largely because of the historic preference of the industry for negotiation or arbitration. However, this historic preference has begun to diminish. This has occurred, at least in part, because some Reinsurers are examining more closely claims which previously would not have received much scrutiny.

from all past, present, and future liability under the reinsurance contract in return for a cash payment); clauses in contract wordings; standstill agreements; and the complexities of underwriting pools. The more specialised a lawyer is in insurance/reinsurance run-off matters the better since his input requires an understanding of the legal complexities together with the practical workings of the marketplace.

Insolvency Practitioner (may be a Liquidator or Scheme Administrator) – Even-handed neutral. Establishes the deficiency of assets in relation to liabilities. In the UK his job is to establish order, realise assets, agree claims, and pay dividends to creditors in priority.

Actuary – A scientist. Estimates the size of liabilities and determines when liabilities are likely to come to an end, based on extrapolation of past data. They are important at all stages of run-off since insolvency is reached at any point when either:

- claims cannot be paid as they fall due;
- assets are less than liabilities.

A good actuary can make or break a company. With regard to commutations, it is widely accepted that estimation and interpretation of reserves is fundamental to negotiating a commutation. Not only are actuaries an obvious choice to add value in this area but also more and more actuaries are taking a lead role at the negotiation table. The most useful actuaries are those which have a good understanding of the technicalities of insurance and reinsurance as well as being competent in their own field.

Commutation expert – The negotiator. The Commutation expert negotiates such **commutations**[vi] with the counterparty. Again, expertise in this area can be invaluable since a company in run-off has limited financial resources.

Accountant – Number cruncher. Keeps the financial books and files returns. He estimates the assets available.

Third Party Run-off managers – Agents of the insurance/reinsurance company appointed to administer the book of business. There are two distinct types – the passive administrator and the

(vi) **Expiry** of a risk issued on a loss-occurring basis takes place when there is no longer any liability under the contract. In practical terms, this is when a long period has elapsed since the last claim has been advised. In legal terms liability may continue. Therefore, to ensure legal liability is at an end, the risk should be **extinguished** by agreement. Such an agreement is called a **commutation** and represents cash payment by the Insurer/Reinsurer for his release from liability.

aggressive problem-solver. He may attempt to extinguish liabilities arising out of the insurance/reinsurance contracts depending upon the contractual incentives available. If paid by the transaction, he has little incentive to shorten the run-off period. If paid by results he may take a different approach.

Consultant – Trouble-shooter. Advises on reinsurance technical matters throughout; he has an intimate knowledge of the workings of the reinsurance market. Whereas the actuary takes a top-down approach, the consultant offers a bottom-up approach. He can advise on appropriate discontiued business strategies, carry out inspections of records whilst the company is in run-off; and validate claims presentations for Schemes of Arrangement. He takes a practical and informal approach to the problem, often cutting through a lot of the red tape that can be involved. The best consultants are akin to management consultants, the worst to estate agents, since they have no regulatory body.

Brokers – Intermediary. He places the protection and then collects the claims as they arise. Without the co-operation and support of the Broker, the company in run-off has a higher probability of becoming insolvent. In the London Market, the Broker holds the ace card since he holds a lot of the original claims information in his paper records and collects reinsurance recoveries for the company in run-off. Since the reinsurance programme is often the run-off entity's major asset, the importance of the Broker cannot be overstated. Despite this, most companies in run-off cannot bring themselves to pay the Broker an additional reinsurance claims collection fee because they feel that he is morally not entitled to one, having received brokerage on the premium at the outset.

Regulator (FSA) – Big Brother. He acts on behalf of the government to ensure that the company does not become insolvent or prejudice the rights of the policyholders at any time. Must be consulted at every step of the way to ensure that he is happy with any proposals. There is little point conducting any sort of major restructuring plans without consulting the FSA first to get their opinion.

To understand the run-off industry it is first necessary to understand some basics of the reinsurance[vii] industry and beneath that

(vii) Reinsurance can be defined in simple terms as 'the insurance of insurance companies'. Just as individuals seek to cover themselves against the financial risks inherent in every day life (such as the costs of a car accident) so Insurers seek protection against their liabilities under the policies they have issued.

the insurance industry. For many people the term run-off is a term that has no real meaning, little attempt is made to prise open its connotations and associations. It is for many people a dull subject since it does not have the razzmatazz of the underwriting operation, it does not make a profit and it exists at the tail end of an insurance operation's existence. Run-off is important, it can and should be dynamic but as with most things it requires a certain amount of expertise and professionalism which is sadly lacking in many organisations which carry it out. The reason for this in general terms is that almost all run-off organisations have become such by default. That is to say, they have grown out of insurance/reinsurance operations that have been put into discontinuation mode. They have not been founded as a specialist run-off operator with its core activity and area of expertise being the provision of run-off services. As such, the number of true run-off professionals is limited. This is also significant in that the mindset required to be a run-off professional is poles apart from that required for an insurance/reinsurance professional working in the on-going business sector. Different skills and attributes are demanded. It is critical for the insurance/reinsurance industry to find better solutions to the problems of run-off in order to operate more effectively as an industry in a period when alternatives to traditional reinsurance are beginning to gain a foothold[viii]. This book will attempt to place run-off within a context, which is at once clear and logical, and portrays its significance in terms of the huge liabilities at stake (in a recent survey by a Reinsurer, it was estimated that the liabilities of run-off companies world-wide presently stood at $230 billion and this would rise to $505 billion by 2006) and the modern methods developed to cope with this problem.

In essence, the process of running off the liability of a portfolio of business begins when the insurance/reinsurance organisation decides to close its doors and to stop writing new business. Critically, liability to pay the claims arising under insurance and reinsurance policies does not stop – if it did, there would be no run-off industry. From the point of going into run-off the company turns into a 'claims paying machine' and a change of emphasis is called for. An Underwriter in an on-going company focuses on underwriting aims, such as volume, market share, premiums, and reported profits. A company in run-off will focus on:

- reducing costs;
- centralising credit control;

(viii) Alternatives to reinsurance are referred to generically as alternative risk transfer and are considered later in this book.

- extinguishing liabilities through the use of commutations.

In order to achieve each of these central aims there are a large number of activities and processes which must be put in place. The core activities consist of valuing assets and liabilities, managing the inwards claims and reinsurance recoveries, investing and commuting. Run-offs have a much greater emphasis on cashflow. The simple reason is that, other than the cash generated from its claims, reinsurance recoveries and investment performance, there is no alternative revenue stream and, indeed, no access to additional capital (except in very rare circumstances from a parent company).

Run-offs require a change in attitude and approach as compared to operating an ongoing company.

The uniqueness of the insurance/reinsurance product

To put run-off into context, it should be noted that the (re)insurance product itself is *unique* in that its quality can only be judged when something goes wrong. It involves the delayed performance of a contractual promise to pay claims. Insurance/reinsurance companies therefore act as guarantors of other company's financial risks, and regulation is needed to ensure that insurance/reinsurance companies keep their side of the bargain. Such regulation is provided by the Financial Services Authority ("**FSA**") as **Regulator** of the insurance/reinsurance industry.

The importance of market practice

It is necessary to understand that the insurance/reinsurance industry has developed both formal and informal methods of operation so that the strict contractual obligations are often overlooked (although not ignored) in the interests of achieving commercial objectives. An understanding of market practice is essential in understanding the insurance/reinsurance industry.

Reinsurance is a transaction whereby the Reinsurer, for payment of a premium, agrees to indemnify (i.e. compensate) the insurance company against all or part of the loss which the insurance company may suffer under a policy or policies that it has issued.[ix]

(ix) The Role of Reinsurance – Reinsurance serves a vital role in the insurance industry. Through reinsurance, an Insurer is able to spread the risk on a policy or classes of policies reinsured and lessen its exposure to catastrophic losses. Reinsurance also enables an Insurer to reduce the amount of reserves usually required

continued overleaf

The different interests of the stakeholders

An active insurance company has a primary duty to shareholders (being the owners) and to other stakeholders (being other parties with an interest in the company, such as Employees, Contract Workers, Management, Regulators, Brokers, etc.). A company in run-off on the other hand, arguably has a primary duty to its creditors i.e. policyholders (with shareholders being a close second). Regulation exists to enforce this duty. In the UK the Financial Services Authority

---

by law. By providing indemnity to insurance companies for a portion of their risk, reinsurance allows the insurance companies to accept greater amounts of risk without impairing their capital. See R.Carter *Reinsurance.*

In exchange for reinsuring a portion of the risk, the Reinsurer is paid a premium based on the amount and type of risk underwritten. Because the reinsured is responsible for the overhead associated with insuring the risk, e.g. marketing, underwriting and claims handling, the premium paid to the Reinsurer is less than that received by the Reinsured from the Insured.

Reinsurance may be effectuated either by treaty or by facultative agreement. A reinsurance treaty is an agreement between a Reinsured and a Reinsurer, usually for one year or longer, which stipulates some class or classes of business that will automatically be covered by the agreement. Facultative reinsurance is a separately negotiated, discrete coverage indemnifying the Reinsured with respect to all or part of a particular risk.

Utmost good faith – the relationship between a Reinsurer and a Reinsured is contractual in nature and generally governed by the duty of utmost good faith. Utmost good faith, has been defined by one commentator (*Reinsurance*, R.Strain), as follows: "Utmost good faith speaks to fair dealing. On the one hand, it legitimises an agreement to perform routine reformation of mere technical and inadvertent errors in the ceding of ' reinsurance under treaties before and after loss, but rejects a unilateral decision to cede a larger cession after a loss than would have been made before it. On the other hand, good faith is not a shelter against the bad judgement or carelessness of either party. Yet it frequently animates an agreement to cancel or reform when reinsurance is shown to be manifestly unfair or unreasonably burdensome to either party, regardless of reason or fault. A party to a reinsurance contract is expected to go outside the literal terms of an agreement in any situation, if necessary, to enforce the original meeting of the minds. And that meeting of the minds must have been accomplished within a full and complete exercise of good faith."

Judicial standards applied to the enforcement of the duty of utmost good faith have generally been dependent upon the specific obligation of the Reinsured at issue, for example, a Reinsured' s duty to provide underwriting information, duty to provide timely notice of claims, or duty to defend.

Privity of contract between Insured and Reinsurer – the relationships among a Reinsurer, a Reinsured and an Insured are governed by the contracts between them. The Reinsurer's obligations are defined by the reinsurance contract, the terms of the insurance policy reinsured, and by the duty of utmost good faith that underlies the reinsurance relationship. There is ordinarily no privity of contract between the Insured party and the Reinsurer.

provides such regulation, as explained in more detail later in this book.

1.2 The Distinction Between Insurance and Reinsurance

It is important at the outset to be clear about the distinction between insurance and reinsurance. The main differences are that:

- reinsurance is contracted between two industry professionals, rather than a member of the public and a professional. As such, technical jargon is used in the contract and certain assumptions are made regarding the extent of the other party's knowledge during the administration of the liabilities under the contract. This can create problems for parties trying to understand the nature of the contract because of the informal market practices adopted in its execution;
- reinsurance arrangements tend to be more complex than those of insurance, and often include multiple layers of protection (known as **retrocession**[x], or reinsurance of reinsurance business);
- certain practices in reinsurance are so distinct that the insurance supervisory authorities (i.e. FSA) regard them as a separate class;

These differences have consequences for the management of an operation in run-off in terms of:

- the cost of administering the run-off – the more complex the insurance and reinsurance contracts entered into, the more expensive the run-off tends to be;
- the applicability of certain statutes, e.g. Policyholders Protection Board applies only to insurance and not reinsurance.

1.3 The Definition of 'Run-off'

1.3.1 Company market

The so-called run-off decision is of course mythical. In practice what happens is that a company decides to stop underwriting with the immediate consequence that the company is *de facto* in run-off.

(x) **Retrocession** can be defined in simple terms as 'the reinsurance of reinsurance liabilities'. Just as individuals seek to cover themselves against the financial risks inherent in every day life (such as the costs of a car accident) so Reinsurers seek protection against their liabilities under the reinsurance contracts they have underwritten.

In the UK, **informal 'Run off'** of an insurance/reinsurance company can be defined as:

> "the period of time **from** the Insurer's/Reinsurer's Board of Director's decision to cease the underwriting of risks **until** the time that the last claim under the portfolio of risks underwritten by that insurance/reinsurance entity is paid or the liability under the risks is otherwise brought to a final conclusion."

In simple terms, the liability under each of the policies issued by the company are to be *run-off* until the liability is at an end (either because it has expired or been extinguished). In a traditional run-off an Insurer continues to agree and settle claims until they are all paid.

Arising from this definition, it should be noted that:

- there is no legal definition of run-off;
- there is no statutory obligation to announce the decision, although this is almost always done in practice. It is generally announced to the shareholders and the general public alike via a press release. In most cases the decision to withdraw from active underwriting takes immediate effect;
- the term 'run-off' is simply a description of an insurance/reinsurance company's current **trading status** (whether relative to the company as a whole or just a particular portfolio of business, for which, see below). Once it has obtained a licence to transact a certain class of insurance business a company can only be in one of four modes (whether relative to the company as a whole or just a particular portfolio of business):
    - not yet operational;
    - a live company – i.e. still writing new (and renewal) business;
    - a company in run-off – i.e. has ceased writing new (and renewal) business;
    - an insolvent company[xi] (in liquidation or a Scheme of Arrangement) i.e. it has insufficient assets to meet its liabilities.

(xi) Due to the fact that Insurers/Reinsurers are monitored internally by the management and externally *inter alia* by the rating agencies; the FSA; shareholders; and investment analysts it is very rare that an Insurer or Reinsurer goes from being a live company to becoming insolvent and going into liquidation. However, it is possible and it does occur on occasions, as shown in the recent case of Black Sea and Baltic.

In the UK, **formal 'Run off'** of an insurance/reinsurance company can be defined as:

> "the period of time **from** the Insurer's/Reinsurer's Board of Director's application to the **FSA** to have its licences revoked[xii] **until** the time that the last claim under the portfolio of risks underwritten by that insurance/reinsurance entity is paid or the liability under the risks is otherwise brought to a final conclusion."

It should be noted that:

- the process of going into run-off, whether formal or informal, and the fact that a company is in run-off is **not** necessarily a reflection of the insurance/reinsurance company's financial strength. This is an important conceptual distinction and should be borne in mind whenever reference to the term 'run-off' is made: financial grounds are only one of many factors involved in the decision to go into run-off and indeed may not be a factor at all in certain circumstances. Perversely, it is possible that a company's financial strength can actually increase after being placed into run-off. This is the current situation (as at January 2001) at the biggest run-off company in the world – Equitas – although it is accepted that it is very early days in the development of that particular company.[xiii] In general, however, it is often the case that there is *some correlation* between the process of going into run-off and the company's financial strength. Indeed, rating agencies (which are concerned with assessing a company's financial health and claims-paying ability) may downgrade the rating of an Insurance/Reinsurance entity which is put into run-off. This may be based upon such reasons as the fact that the company which is part of a group of companies does not appear to be strategically important to the group of companies as a whole and to reflect the lone company's stand-alone financial strength;
- the term 'run-off' stops being applied to a company upon the company being put into a **Scheme of Arrangement**[xiv] (whether a solvent or insolvent scheme) or becoming **insolvent**. In both of these cases the liabilities are no longer run-off until expiry. Rather, under a Scheme of Arrangement the creditors agree to receive a

(xii) However, the seeking of the revocation of licences is not obligatory and it has only recently (in 1999) been introduced as FSApolicy to enforce it.

(xiii) While in the short term Equitas is on track it is important not to lose sight of the inherent uncertainties in Equitas' business, and in particular of its long-tail asbestos, pollution and health hazards related liabilities. These may ultimately lead to it paying only a percentage of each claim presented rather than 100%.

(xiv) Under section 425 of the Companies Act 1985.

reduced percentage payout of their losses and the liabilities are consequently finalised. Under insolvency the liabilities are administered under statute by an insolvency practitioner who calculates the percentage payout of the losses based upon the deficiency of the total assets in relation to the total liabilities. The main difference between these two eventualities is that creditors have some form of control (via their voting rights) under a Scheme of Arrangement, but it is the liquidator who has the control under liquidation. Furthermore a Scheme of Arrangement is a more flexible tool than the dogmatic approach encapsulated within the administration of a liquidation.

It should be noted that companies going into run-off need to make major changes in their focus and approach. The table below outlines eight of the key changes. A deeper analysis of this issue is dealt with later in the book.

Company in run-off	On-going company
Main goals: financial FINALITY i.e. return capital to shareholders and avoid insolvency at all costs	*Main goal: make a profit and increase long-term shareholder value.*
Emphasis on claims	*Emphasis on underwriting*
Purpose: to collect reinsurance claims and distribute funds to policyholders	*Purpose: to underwrite new insurance/ reinsurance business*
Major asset is often potential reinsurance recoveries	*Major asset is capital*
Focus on reinsurance recoveries, expense control	*Focus on premium income*
Legal points often taken on terms and conditions of policies insured/reinsured (leading to savings on inward claims)	*Legal points often* not *taken on terms and conditions of policies for commercial reasons*
Staff skills required relate to processing business (especially claims); managing liabilites; and negotiating commutations	*Staff skills required relate to competing for new business by monitoring service levels and innovation*
In theory at least, creditors (i.e. policyholders) interests are paramount due to the scrutiny of the FSA.	*Shareholders interests are paramount*
Views of FSA very important	*Views of* FSA *of less significance although still of importance*

Table 1 – Key changes required in the focus and approach of companies going into run-off.

1.3.2 Distinction Between Partial and Complete Run-off

We need draw a distinction between, the situation where:

1. Only some parts of the insurance/reinsurance company business goes into run-off; and
2. The whole entity ceases to underwrite.

We must differentiate the following:

- an Insurance/Reinsurance *group* going into run-off;
- insurance/Reinsurance *company (which is part of a group)* going into run-off;
- insurance/Reinsurance *company (which is* ***not part of a group****)* going into run-off;
- insurance/Reinsurance *portfolio* going into run-off;
- insurance/Reinsurance company *branch* going into run-off.

1.3.2.1 An Insurance/Reinsurance group

It is quite common to see companies formed into groups consisting of a **parent company** (also known as a **holding company**) which owns a number of **subsidiary companies**. The functions of the holding company may be limited to managing its subsidiaries that in turn run the underlying businesses. Under section 736 of the Companies Act 1985,a company is a *subsidiary* of another company if it's holding company:

(1) holds a majority of the *voting rights*[xv] in it, or

(2) is a member of it and has the right to appoint or remove a majority of its board of directors[xvi], or

---

(xv) Voting rights mean the rights conferred on shareholders to vote at general meetings of the company on all or substantially all matters. Accordingly, votes attaching to securities such as preference shares, which confer voting rights only where the matters to be decided relate to the interest of preference shareholders, are disregarded.

(xvi) References to the right to appoint or remove 'a majority'of the board of directors mean directors together holding a majority of the rights to vote at meetings of the board; again on all, or substantially all matters. A company is not regarded as having 'the right to appoint a director' if that right is exercisable only with the consent or concurrence of another person. However, a company is deemed to have the right to appoint a director if that person's appointment flows necessarily from his appointment as a director of the holding company or if the directorship is held by the holding company itself.

(3) is a member of it and controls alone, pursuant to an agreement with other shareholders or members, a majority of the *voting rights* in it, or

(4) it is a subsidiary of a company which is itself a subsidiary of the *holding company*.

The attraction of operating through a group of companies rather than divisions of a single company has much to do with the fact that each company within the group is a separate legal entity with limited liability. The parent company, for example, is not liable for the debts of its subsidiaries unless it has agreed to assume responsibility for them or there are other special circumstances.

An Insurance/Reinsurance group is simply a group of insurance/reinsurance companies under the common control of a holding company. Where there is a group of insurance/reinsurance companies it is likely that due to their size and the principles underlying risk, that they will underwrite a diverse account i.e. various classes of insurance/reinsurance business spread geographically. Because of this, and taking into account the reasons why companies go into run-off (discussed below), it is unlikely that a whole group (i.e. all the constituent member companies forming that group) will simultaneously go into run-off either voluntarily or otherwise. This is because one of the main reasons for going into run-off is the unprofitability of the business and it is unlikely that a large number of various classes spread geographically will experience problems at exactly the same time. However, a comprehensive withdrawal from the insurance/reinsurance industry is possible. One example may be where the insurance group is itself part of a larger group of companies, and the parent company decides that insurance/reinsurance is no longer a **core business** and therefore wishes to withdraw from the whole industry.

A good example of this was the Xerox Corporation's announcement that it was moving out of financial services to concentrate on its document processing business. In 1993 the company separated the Crum & Forster Group into seven operating companies each with more focused business purposes, and created an offshore reinsurance entity to provide additional reinsurance protection to each of the entities. Since that date, Xerox has sold all seven of the individual companies.

In effect, the parent has decided that he can more profitably use his capital elsewhere – the increasing focus of corporate entities upon the return on capital and shareholder value may be a catalyst in this direction. Another example may be where the group consists of a small number of companies, say three, and their writings are not particularly diverse. Consequently they may all have been adversely affected by the same or similar **loss events** (such as a major hurricane).

1.3.2.2 Insurance/Reinsurance company which is itself part of a group

This case of an **Insurance/Reinsurance company which is itself part of a group**, which decides, or is forced, to go into run-off is distinct. We are concerned here with the scenario where other members of the group continue to write business in the normal way and are largely unaffected by the placing into run-off of one of the group members.

Where such a move is a conscious restructuring to segregate the run-off of discontinued (often long-tailed) liabilities, from the liabilities relating to current ongoing business, some of the business reasons why it is carried out are as follows:

1. To improve financial results for the current ongoing business by conclusively *quantifying* the old liabilities and segregating them for run-off.
2. To gain competitive advantage – by quantifying the old liabilities that are resulting in a drag on earnings, a company can allocate capital to address the pre-existing liabilities, thereby freeing the remaining surplus for allocation to the on-going operation. In addition to surplus allocation, more specialised management and personnel allocations can be made. With these changes, it is likely that more favourable ratings will be assigned to the on-going company that helps to attract new capital and improve market position.

Possible repercussions for groups that carry out such restructuring include:

- a psychological tarnishing of the **brand name** of the group and loss of valuable goodwill in the eyes of the insurance/reinsurance community who often view entrance into run-off as a cause of some concern. This is mainly because it has been the history of certain companies in run-off that they have not honoured their obligations to respond to claims as well as could have been expected. Whether any tarnishing occurs will depend heavily upon the individual circumstances surrounding the reasons for placing the company into run-off and the reputation of the company for responding to claims in good faith;

- the downgrading of the Insurance/Reinsurance Company which is put into run-off by the various rating agencies. This may be based upon such reasons as the fact that the company does not appear to be strategically important to the group and reflecting the lone company's stand-alone financial strength. (Note that each company that is part of a group is a separate legal entity).

1.3.2.3 Insurance/Reinsurance Company, which is not part of a group

In the case of a single Insurance/Reinsurance company, **which is not part of a group**, which decides, or is forced, to go into run-off there is no **possibility** of a future capital injection from a parent company (arising from possible intra-group financial guarantees or letters of support).[xvii] Furthermore, any possible transfer of any ongoing business of the company to third parties (subject to approval by the Financial Services Authority) will require a due diligence review by the third party and this may hamper the practicalities of successfully transferring the business given that speed is very important in such circumstances (because of the need to administer ongoing policies and renew policies as the old ones expire). In the case where there is a simple agreement that another company will be allowed the rights of renewing the business previously written by the company now in run-off this will not be a problem: there is no risk for the new Insurer/Reinsurer – he can simply write the risks in the normal fashion.

Again, depending upon the individual circumstances surrounding the reasons for placing the company into run-off the company may be subject to a downgrading of its credit rating.

1.3.2.4 Insurance/Reinsurance portfolio

As explained above, an Insurance/Reinsurance entity may write a large variety of classes of business. Due to various factors, it may decide to withdraw from a certain class of business, such as marine business, but

(xvii) It should be noted that the possibility of a future capital injection from a parent company in respect of a company that is part of a group does not arise from a legal obligation. As noted above, each company within the group is a separate legal entity with limited liability. The parent company, for example, is not liable for the debts of its subsidiaries unless it has agreed to assume responsibility for them or there are other special circumstances.

carry on writing other classes such as non-marine. This is known as putting a portfolio (of business) into run-off. An example of this occurred in July 1995 when Zurich Re (UK), the London market arm of Continental European insurance giant, the Zurich Group, announced it had ceased writing *aviation reinsurance business* with immediate effect. In this case, the announcement affected some 45% of the Zurich Re (UK)'s aviation business. According to Insurance Day at the time:

"The withdrawal from aviation reinsurance business was prompted by the negative results which the account has been suffering in recent years and the London market insurer's view that, looking forward, there is little prospect for such business to produce the type of sustained profits which are required to make it worthwhile writing such volatile business.

Zurich Re (UK) added that it has achieved substantial capital growth in other areas of its business such as the property and casualty account and could see better prospects coming from such sectors."

Depending upon the significance of the portfolio to the company concerned in terms of premium income; and the exact reasons for the company to put the portfolio into run-off, such a move may not be viewed negatively by the insurance/reinsurance industry. It is regarded as a simple fact of life that the industry is cyclical and that as underwriting profits decrease over the cycle certain companies will disappear from the marketplace. Likewise, new companies would be expected to enter the market once conditions have improved. Moreover, since the company is active in other areas of insurance/reinsurance it is likely that the company has made profits elsewhere. Critically, its desire to maintain good business relations in the industry as a whole will generally lead it to conduct the run-off of the account on an "orderly basis" – a code word for the *payment of valid claims as they fall due.* All parties are clear that the possibility of a future cash injection to support the portfolio in run-off theoretically exists. Any capital injections which do occur, and they are rare, tend to take place at the beginning of the run-off.

1.3.2.5 Insurance/Reinsurance Company branch

Insurance/Reinsurance Company branch going into run-off – this, in effect, is a withdrawal from a country. An example of this occurred in June 1997, when the Gloucester-based company East West Insurance, which had a portfolio of 200,000 private cars, was put into run-off. Its main shareholder was unhappy with the returns it was getting from the business. According to Insurance Day at the time:

"UK Insurer East West is pulling out of the personal lines market and going into run-off, claiming the UK motor sector is too competitive to give shareholders a decent return.. The company, 90% owned by Malaysia's Sime Derby Berhad, purely writes personal lines business and distributes its products solely via intermediaries. East West is ceasing to quote for new business from today. It will continue to process quotes in the pipeline up to June 30. Lloyd's agency Equity Red Star has concluded a deal with East West to offer renewal terms to policyholders, from July. A company statement yesterday stressed that East West was still solvent. "The decision [to go into run off] is strategic and not dictated by the current asset levels of the company," it said. "Fierce competition prevalent in the UK market has prohibited the company from providing a reasonable expectation of an appropriate return to shareholders." East West employs 122 people who face the prospect of gradual redundancy."

1.3.3 Lloyd's syndicates

Lloyd's syndicates are a special case and do not fall neatly into the above categories due to the unique nature of the Lloyd's market. This comprises a large number of separate and independent managing agents, who provide a diversity of expertise for the conduct of international insurance and reinsurance business. Members of Lloyd's, both corporate and individual provide the underwriting capacity that is managed by the agents. The members are authorised to underwrite insurance both in the UK and in about 60 overseas jurisdictions. The businesses in the market are supported by a common infrastructure offering technical expertise, information exchange and an efficient processing capability. The market operates a common security system with members satisfying a common solvency standard. It is underpinned by the Central Fund, which is available to meet losses should any member be unable to pay its share of losses.

Business is accepted through a Lloyd's syndicate. Historically, this has been a group of members on whose behalf a managing agent accepts insurance business, although in recent years there has been a move to syndicates being supported by a single corporate member.

The key features of traditionally organised Lloyd's syndicates are:

- a member commits to provide an amount of underwriting capacity which is normally allocated to a number of different syndicates;

- the syndicate for any year of account consists of the capacity allocated to it by members. A syndicate is an annual venture. Each member of a syndicate underwrites insurance contracts on its own behalf (i.e. with several liability only);
- the managing agent of a syndicate employs and manages the Underwriter and underwriting team. They in turn accept risks, pay claims, arrange reinsurance, close the account through a reinsurance to close and strike a profit or loss on the year's trading on the members' behalf;
- a syndicate normally closes the account for each year's underwriting 36 months after its commencement. The profit or loss declared for that year's trading is audited and is distributed to or collected from the members of the syndicate via the premiums trust funds; and
- a syndicate will normally re-form from year to year and members for a particular year of account will generally reinsure (in return for a premium) the unexpired liabilities of the members of the syndicate during the immediately preceding year, i.e. the **reinsurance to close**. Upon payment of the premium the preceding year of account is closed.

Run-off Accounts

Where it is not possible to close an account owing to material uncertainties, e.g. it is not possible to assess ultimate losses and arrive at a figure for the reinsurance to close, the year of account must be left open as long as necessary. In such cases the term used is 'run-off'.

Diagram 2 – The legal and financial position of a company in run-off

This diagram shows the flow of liabilities and cash into and out of a company in run-off. The main source of income is the potential reinsurance recoveries and investment income (invested to meet the expected payout pattern of the incoming claims).

Insolvency occurs where (a) the company is unable to meet its debt as they fall due or (b) liabilities exceed or may exceed (see Insolvency Act) available assets – Insolvency Act 1986. Therefore, the efficient recovery of potential reinsurance recoveries and the accurate estimation of liabilities are crucial.

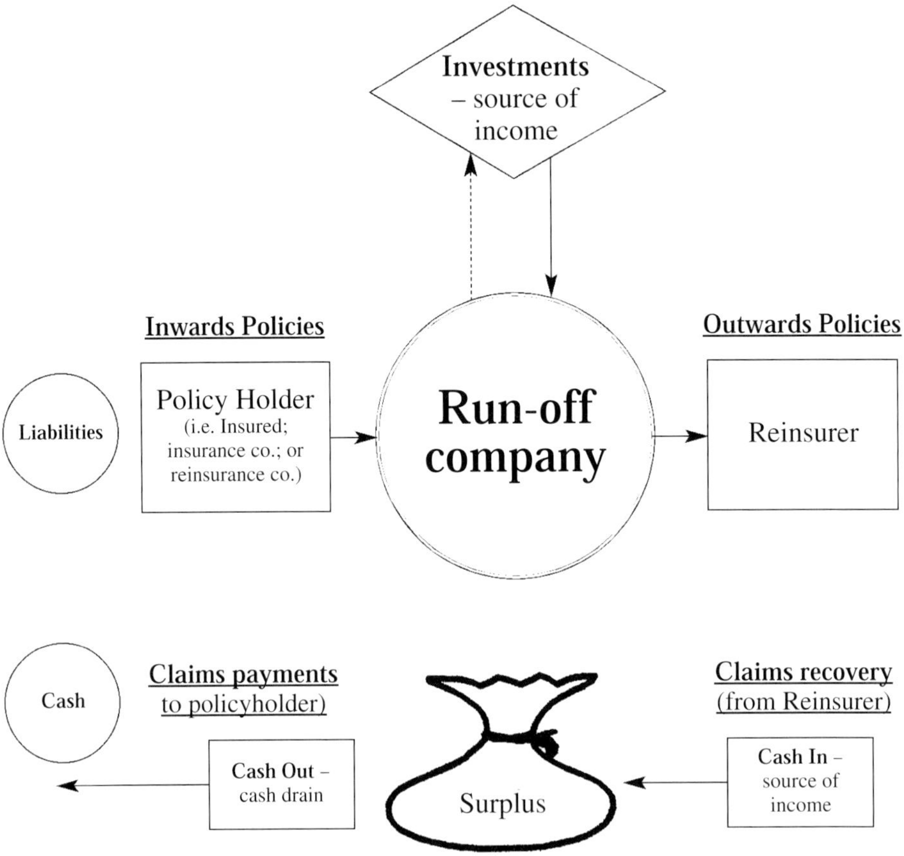

CHAPTER 2: BACKGROUND

Current intense competition and soft premiums, volatile equity markets and potential catastrophes on the horizon have created almost perfect insolvency conditions. The value of the world-wide run-off market, currently at more than 20% of total liabilities of insurance and reinsurance companies, is sure to rise.

This chapter will examine the growth of the run-off market and trends in the insurance/reinsurance industry in order to better understand its current and future needs. By way of background, Britain is the fourth largest market in the world (after the USA, Japan and Germany) in respect of live business.

2.1 Growth of the Run-off Market

2.1.1 Past growth

The run-off industry first emerged as a recognised 'business' over 25 years ago – around the mid 1970's. Since that time it has grown from an industry pertaining to millions of dollars to one concerning billions.

The industry has been exposed to a large variety of forces in the past two decades. Some influencing factors were company-specific and took the form of mispriced liabilities, for example, or of mergers and acquisitions. Others, such as asset value volatility, emerged in response to changes in interest, exchange and inflation rates. At the same time, structural changes came about through globalisation, regulation and deregulation trends. During the 1980's and early 1990's huge claims were notified regarding asbestos-related, pollution and health hazard risks emanating principally from the United States. The rate of insolvencies and Insurers going into run-off in the mid-1980s/early 1990s, which ensued amongst old established companies, especially in the London Market, was unprecedented.

Run-off has been one of the insurance sector's big growth areas in the last couple of decades. Curiously, however, the industry itself has been very slow in responding to the changing circumstances.

2.1.2 Future growth

In the sphere of general insurance, some commentators see the continued growth of the run-off industry (including insolvencies) due to changes in:

The demand for insurance and reinsurance

- as a result of increasing customer sophistication, with customers seeking a broader range of services and innovative products (such as multi-year/multi-line contracts) there is a reduced demand for the traditional reinsurance product. There is a move towards higher risk retentions and seeking reinsurance with reinsurers of a certain minimum capital size;
- the restructuring of the Broker industry, with the most dramatic illustration being the rapid consolidation among major global groups. Allied to this is the internal reorganisations within these large Brokers which is concentrating placement decisions for many lines of business into a small number of key offices. Again, Brokers are segmenting their portfolio and directing specific classes of business to small panels of preferred Reinsurers with large capital bases;
- the demand for insurance in the largest markets, the USA, Europe, and Japan, is stagnant. On a historical basis, the growth of net written premium in the USA at only 2.6% in 1999[i] is 0.7% below the average of the last 10 years.

Supply of insurance and reinsurance

- there is market consolidation and globalisation of the major reinsurance players resulting in stronger capital bases – such a trend tends to squeeze out those Reinsurers with weaker capital bases;
- intensification of competition, from domestic carriers in markets such as the US which are successfully capturing market share from the London market, and from relatively new markets such as Bermuda which has taken a major share in segments such as property excess of loss reinsurance;
- consequently premiums are extremely soft. Over-capacity in all the world's mature economies, sees rates driven lower and lower in almost every class of business.

In summary, the intense competition and low premiums do not augur well for the future. In addition, many Insurers are reaping the results of what has turned out to be under-priced cover in the past, with the result that ultimate claims will exceed income.

(i) (Source – property and causality, predictions for 1999 net written premiums)

Current expert opinion

Among those predicting growth in the number of companies in run-off are the credit-rating agency AM Best and the Reinsurer Swiss Re.

As a rough approximation we can assess the continued growth of the run-off market by reference to a study on insurance insolvency by AM Best. If we look at the reasons why companies go insolvent, we see some interesting trends and of more importance some clear parallels with the current market. AM Best produced a special report in February 1999 which posed the question: "Insolvency: Will historic trends return?" As we can see from the table below, the number of US insolvencies over the last 25 years has been substantial, with the period between 1985 and the early 1990's displaying the greatest frequency. During this latter period the insolvency rate was approximately 2% by number of the companies operating in the market at that time.

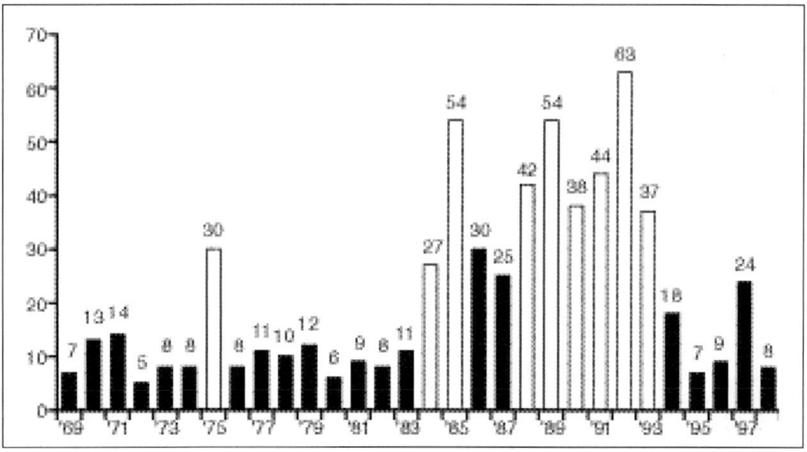

Table 2: Number of Property/Casualty Insolvencies in the US by year
Source: A M Best:

The AM Best study identified a number of key reasons why companies become insolvent. The primary causes were identified as:

- deficient reserves;
- inadequate pricing combined with rapid growth

In addition some other root causes were:

- catastrophes in the period 1989-93 caused 20 insolvencies in the US;
- asset failure including the impact of reinsurance failure;

- marked shifts in business mix.

As highlighted above the global insurance and reinsurance market at present is characterised by intense competition and extremely soft premiums. In addition, equity markets are volatile at present thereby undermining investment returns. Reinsurers' results have been propped up by reserve releases over the past few years and on the horizon we have potential natural and man-made catastrophes. Taken together it appears that we have **almost perfect insolvency conditions**.

Longer-term, AM Best expects insolvencies to rise.[ii]

A Swiss Re study published in 1998 looked at what they called the "run-off phenomenon"[iii]. However, the source for all figures regarding the size of the run-off market was the management consultants McKinsey & Company Inc. It was indicated that the run-off market was set to grow at 10% per annum (with the growth rates in internal run-off portfolios at 15%) owing to deregulation of the insurance industry in continental Europe.

2.1.3 Consolidation in the insurance and reinsurance market

As noted briefly above, as a consequence of competition and a flat demand, both the insurance and reinsurance market is consolidating. In the 1990's, American Reinsurers bought into the European markets including the acquisition of Cologne Re by General Re, and the purchase of Frankona Re by Employers Re. Unprecedented consolidation in the reinsurance industry was also seen elsewhere with Munich Re acquiring American Re, Swiss Re acquiring M&G and Scor acquiring Allstate's reinsurance interests. Consolidation is fuelled by:

- companies looking to achieve economies of scale and to complement the apparent strengths of each partner;
- a desire to diversify and expand into different market places;
- more specifically, a desire to maintain margins by reducing expenses.

The past decade has seen the number of domestic US Reinsurers halve to about sixty.

(ii) AM Best, Special Report, February 1999, Insolvency: *Will Historic Trends Return?*

(iii) Swiss Re *The run-off phenomenon – Extracting value from discontinued business* 1998

A.M. Best think that this could shrink by another ten to twenty in the future. With a trend towards bigger shares, smaller Reinsurers are facing a widening gap between the "haves" and the "have-nots". With an increasing flight to quality and with increasing requirements of surplus levels putting pressure on ratings, there will only be a further polarisation into the strong and the weak

Equally the scale of losses resulting from natural catastrophes since the late 1980s means that Reinsurers now are expected to have the financial resources and capital strength to meet large, sudden, claims payments.

2.1.4 The effect of the consolidation on the size of the run-off market

At present, it should be noted that

- four dominant insurance groups (Munich Re, Swiss Re, General Re and Employers Re) write more than one third of world wide reinsurance business; and
- the 25 largest companies or groups account for nearly 66%[iv],

Assuming that there are 9,000 world-wide writing Reinsurers (of which 4,000 are captive insurers) this means that 8,975 (9000 less the 25 above) are competing for 33% of the business. There are simply too many companies chasing too little business at too low a price.

Increasing consolidation in the reinsurance market will likely lead to more small carriers being unable to survive.

Based on past trends, an increasing rate of reinsurance failure will itself lead to further Reinsurer failures, since the market is so incestuous, with each Reinsurer reinsuring each other (however, this problem is not so pronounced outside of London). According to Best's, reinsurance failure has been one of the primary causes of insolvency (being the cause in 5% of all insolvencies in the period 1969-1998)[v]. This factor was particularly prevalent in the mid-1980's. This is a period known as one in which Reinsurers partook in cash-flow underwriting.

We can summarise the factors likely to lead to an increase in run-off in the future as:

(iv) Moody's Investor Services, September 1998

(v) AM Best, Special Report, February 999, *Insolvency: Will Historic Trends Return?*

- a high level of competition;
- an increased trend towards consolidation;
- deregulation.

In short, **run-off will grow** as certain Insurers and Reinsurers are unable to compete in the new environment.

2.2 The Size of the Discontinued Insurance Market

2.2.1 Introduction

The actual **size** of the run-off market is uncertain due to the fact that a large part of the run-off market is run-off in-house which is difficult to quantify. However, it can be said with certainty that there has been a rapid and extensive **growth** in the recent past.

After looking at the market globally, we analyse below the size of the market in two of the principal markets, being the USAand the UK. There are several sources of data for the current size of the market. However, hard and fast data is hard to come by and estimates are often the best that can be supplied.

2.2.2 Global size

2.2.2.1 Estimates of global run-off gross liabilities

2.2.2.1.1 Estimates of global run-off gross liabilities vary, as follows:

Year	General Insurers – Run-Off Global Gross Liabilities in US$ Billion	
	Mckinsey estimate	Chiltington estimate[vi]
1996		220
1998	230	
2001	350	
2006	505	

Table 3 – Estimates of global run-off gross liabilities.

(vi) *Run-off, a solvable problem*, Chiltington Intermediaries Limited – Dr. Wolfgang Eilers/Dr. Hubertus W. Labes

In summary, the best estimate for the late 1990's is in the range US$ 220 billion to US$ 230 billion. Taking the mean average of these figures gives US$ 225 billion.

To put this figure into context, it should be noted that, according to McKinsey, the value of the world-wide run-off market represents more than 20% of total liabilities of insurance companies and over 24% of total liabilities of reinsurance companies in 1998.

Viewed on a world-wide scale, the market is extremely concentrated in only very few countries – namely:

1. USA
2. UK
3. Bermuda
4. Japan[vii]
5. Germany
6. France

These countries account for over 85% of the volume in the worldwide insurance and reinsurance run-off market. The largest element is in the USA where the top 20 reinsurance companies in run-off account for more than 70% of the market.

A more specific estimate of run-off is Chiltington's regional estimate[viii], made in 1996:

Territory	**US$ Billion**	**Share**	**Of which reinsurance**
USA	94	41%	11%
UK	47	21%	50%
Continental Europe	75	33%	25%
Rest of World	4	5%	
Total	**220**	**100%**	N/A

Table 4 – Estimates of regional run-off gross liabilities.

(vii) A particular problem relating to the run-off of companies in Japan is the fact that Reinsurers are unable to post IBNR reserves.

(viii) *Run-off, a solvable problem,* Chiltington Intermediaries Limited.

We can see that the USAhas the bulk of the run-off market arising from the fact that this is the biggest insurance/reinsurance market. Interestingly, the percentage of reinsurance run-off liabilities in the UK, at 50%, is much higher than that illustrated in the US or Continental Europe figures. This arises from the fact that the UK acts as a major international Reinsurer.

2.2.3 UK size

2.2.3.1 Estimates of UK run-off gross liabilities

The largest element of the run-off market in Europe is in the UK. In September 2000, PricewaterhouseCoopers estimated UK run-off gross liabilities to be as follows:

Insurer entity	**US$ Billion**
Insurance company market	39
Equitas Limited	23
Estimated 50 subsidiaries of UK composites plus 50 branch operations in London of foreign parents	16
Total	**78**

Table 5 – Estimates of UK run-off gross liabilities.

This estimate of US$ 78 billion is significantly larger than the US$ 47 billion estimated by Chiltington in 1996 (see Table 4) above since the PricewaterhouseCoopers estimate was made at a later date. Furthermore, such estimation is far from being an exact science.

2.2.3.2 Absolute number of general insurers who have gone into run-off or insolvency

In absolute numbers, as at May 1999 there were **181** companies authorised by the **FSA** in complete run-off in the UK, of which 37 were in some form of formal or informal insolvency process.[ix] To cross-reference this to the estimate of gross liabilities above, 151 of these companies alone account for gross liabilities of £24billion ($39billion). This is according to the UK Treasury's Insurance Directorate.

(ix) Reinsurance, *"Run-Off, Too many cooks spoil the run-off"*, May 1999

2.2.4 USA size

2.2.4.1 Estimates of USA run-off gross liabilities

The only available source of data would appear to be the estimate of US$ **94** billion quoted above. This represented 17% of the gross liabilities of US$ 547 billion of property/casualty Insurers in the USA in 1996.

2.3 A short analysis of particular reasons for going into run-off

2.3.1 Introduction

It should be noted that the reasons for, and the circumstances surrounding, the placing of a company into run-off are so diverse that it is difficult to provide general principles on this point. However, we can focus below upon just four reasons, which have been prevalent in recent years:

- the growth in latent claims (as defined below) during the 1980's and early 1990's;
- catastrophes, particularly in 1989 -1993;
- the insurance cycle.

In the year 1988 for example, companies such as Orion hit financial difficulties thanks to a combination of:

- falling premium rates due to over-capacity in the London market;
- increased notification of asbestos-related claims; and
- losses from catastrophes.

2.3.2 The growth in latent claims

The growth of latent claims during the 1980's and early 1990's led to a number of Insurers and Reinsurers going into run-off, either in whole or in part.

A latent claim can be defined as "A specific type of long-tail liability where there is a **time-lag** between occurrence and manifestation of injury/damage" A dictionary definition of "latent" is something which is "present but not yet fully active; hidden, dormant". In essence then, it is a type of claim where there is a time-lag between cause of loss and its manifestation, for example, a factory worker may be exposed to asbestos products (such as brake linings) in 1951 but might not show any symptoms of illness until 1981. He is ill, but until 1981, he does not know it. As a result of his illness, the worker claims against the company, which employed him back in 1951. That employer looks to the insurance company, which protected him in 1951; and the insurance company in turn, turns to the reinsurance company which provided reinsurance in 1951. Amazingly, claims are still being received in 2001 arising out of exposure to asbestos dust in the 1950's or even earlier. The revenues (premiums) from the sale of those product liability insurance policies flowed through the Insurer's income statements many years ago. However, the expenses (losses and loss adjustment expenses) continue to flow through Insurers' current income statements.

The main types of latent claim are as follows:

- asbestos products leading to asbestos-related diseases[x]. These can lead to both bodily injury and property damage claims;
- environmental pollution, including waste dump sites across the USA;
- pharmaceutical drugs e.g. DES;
- chemical products e.g. Agent Orange;
- lead products leading to lead poisoning;
- tobacco products which result in tobacco-related illnesses;[xi]
- electromagnetic fields ('EMF').[xii]

(x) Between the period 1998 and 2000 an increasing level of claims has driven many asbestos manufacturers to file for bankruptcy. As a result, plaintiffs'lawyers are now looking to sue a broader range of companies not traditionally thought of as asbestos defendants. Consequently, certain Insurers and Reinsurers are increasing their asbestos claims reserves following a rise in filings for potential asbestos claims.

(xi) At present, tobacco is yet to become established as a recognised insurance or reinsurance problem, and tends to be largely dismissed as being unrecoverable.

(xii) At present, EMF is not established as a recognised insurance or reinsurance problem. All lawsuits (except those for loss of value of a property when located next to antennas) have been dismissed for lack of proof of the causal link between bodily injury, property damage, diminution in value of homes (property devaluation)and the EMF. Recent medical and scientific studies are now pointing in the direction of potential problems – recent studies (US, European and Swiss) have come to the conclusion that high levels of cell-phone radiation can cause chromosomal abnormalities in human body cells. However, the FDAare saying that there is still not enough information available.

Despite the lack of success of the lawsuits these cases can have tremendous legal defense costs (in one case this amounted to $10 million).

At present, the first two of these – referred to as asbestos and pollution (or grouped with health hazard claims in general and referred to as 'APH' claims i.e. Asbestos, Pollution and Health Hazard) are easily the most common and of the greatest financial significance.

The reporting of latent claims to reinsurance contracts has grown considerably over the last two decades due in essence to:

- the development of tort law in the USA (relating to asbestos claims); and
- the development of specific and retrospective legislation in the USA (relating to pollution claims).

Whereas, at the time that the risk was written (in the above example being 1951) it is fair to say that such exposures **were not even considered** by the Underwriter, in later years, and in particular the 1980's such claims were held by American courts to be generally recoverable under reinsurance contracts. (However, the London Market has still not accepted the issue of the recoverability of pollution losses, although everyone necessarily reserves for them.) As a result, insurance and reinsurance entities including Lloyd's made huge losses in the late 1980's and early 1990's. In Lloyd's case it lost a total of £7.9 billion in five years, although these losses were caused in part by the LMX[xiii] spiral[xiv], and also coincided with a period of unprecedented insurance and reinsurance catastrophes (see below). Other reinsurance companies writing business emanating from the USA (or, critically, reinsuring other reinsurance companies who themselves had written this business) were affected to a greater or lesser extent around this period or slightly later depending upon:

- the type of business they had written;
- their reinsurance protections;
- the solvency of their Reinsurers;
- what layers of coverage they generally wrote.

(xiii) LMX is an abbreviation for London Market Excess of Loss business

(xiv) A so-called spiral effect occurs when excess of loss Reinsurers extensively underwrite each other's excess of loss protections. This leads to a transfer of exposures to the same players within the market rather than their dispersal outside the market.

2.3.3 Increase in catastrophes

For Insurers and Reinsurers alike, the occurrence of a catastrophe (such as an earthquake) means large, sudden, claims payments. Catastrophes are unpredictable and can be very significant.

A catastrophe is defined by Swiss Re as:

"an occurrence, which claims more than 20 lives, badly injures more than 50 people, makes more than 2000 people homeless or causes insured damage of over $29m or a total loss of over $457m."

A distinction should be drawn between natural and man-made catastrophes. Natural catastrophes are caused by the forces of nature and include such events as:

- earthquakes;
- windstorms;
- hailstorms;
- floods;
- droughts;
- bush fires;
- severe cold weather.

The late 1980's and early 1990's was a period of unprecedented major natural catastrophes such as the UK storms of October 1987 and January 1990 and Hurricane Andrew in August 1992.

After Hurricane Andrew, the number of active Reinsurers fell as many went bankrupt or withdrew from the market. The capacity shortage and the problem of uncollectible debts from insolvent Reinsurers led to much greater importance being attached to the security and rating of Reinsurers[xv]. In short there was a flight to quality i.e. Insurers seeking Reinsurers with large capital bases.

The unprecedented range of catastrophes hitting the London market in the late 1980's and early 1990's is illustrated by the following table produced by LIRMA (London International Insurance and Reinsurance Market Association). The table lists 11 catastrophes, which it deems to be the most important. In descending order they are:

(xv) Source – Swiss Re's economic research department

Catastophe	Date	Gross Loss in the London Market (£m)
Hurricane Hugo	Sept 1987	4,927
European storm	Jan 1990	3,400
Piper Alpha	July 1988	2,743
UK windstorm	Oct 1987	2,002
Hurricane Andrew	August 1992	1,821
Typhoon Mireille	Sept 1991	427
LAeathquake Northridge	Jan 1994	256
Hurricane Imke	Sept 1992	215
St. Mary Axe bomb	April 1992	93
Bishopsgate bomb	April 1993	67
Los Angeles riots	Apr/May 1992	33
	Total	**15,984**

Table 6 – Major catastrophe analysis for the years from October 1987 – December 1993.

2.3.4 The Insurance Cycle

Insurance is naturally a cyclical business – there is a period of low losses and resultant high profits for the industry during which time new players are attracted to the market by the returns, which in the short-term appear very good. With the increased competition resulting from the new entrants, insurance prices tend to fall below that necessary to make an underwriting profit. In short there is too much capacity chasing the business. The traditional response to low rates has been the insurance industry cycle, some Insurers withdraw from the market leaving the rest of the market to increase rates

An example of this occurred in June 1999. As Insurance Day reported at the time:

"AIG has decided to stop underwriting property risks in the London Market and is to place several operations into run-off. The group will stop writing cover through AIG Europe (UK) because of continued poor results, weak rates and overcapacity. In a letter to Brokers, the group said that prospects in the sector 'give us little encouragement. There is simply too much capacity in the property market for rates to increase substantially in the near to medium term'. AIG Europe will continue to write international property cover for UK clients outside the London market."

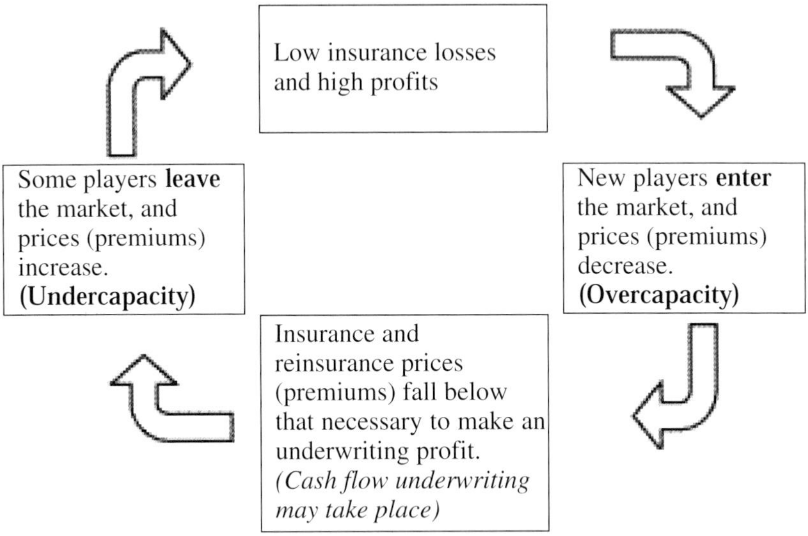

Table 7 – The Insurance Cycle.

Whereas the late 1980's and early 1990's were not a good time for the insurance/reinsurance industry, the period 1994 through 1996 was, in comparison, substantially better. In the last couple of years leading up to 2000, the cycle has turned again into a period of overcapacity and premiums are soft. It is one of the most difficult times pricing-wise which means again that there will be renewed pressures for Insurers and Reinsurers to go into run-off.

According to the management consultants McKinsey, in a European context, "today's declining prices and dwindling volumes are not just the symptoms of another downcycle, rather the entire industry map is being redrawn"[xvi]. In short, Mckinsey view the current downturn as a paradigm shift towards (re)insurance products being bought from large players with large capital bases.

As can be seen from the short analysis above, once extraordinary events, such as an unprecedented string of catastrophes, are superimposed upon the natural insurance cycle, the probability of Insurers and Reinsurers going into run-off is significantly increased. The late 1980's and early 1990's period saw such a convergence of circumstances, and it is possible that something like this could happen again. The three biggest potential challenges facing the market at the moment are arguably:

(xvi) McKinsey *Quarterly Commercial Lines insurance in Europe,* Quarterly 1997

- a major catastrophe occurring in a highly populated; high value; highly insured environment, such as an earthquake hitting the centre of Los Angeles;
- the tobacco litigation. (At present, this is yet to become established as a recognised reinsurance problem, and tends to be largely dismissed as being unrecoverable);[xvii] and
- the threat of global warming with its attendant consequences.

2.4 Case Study of Entry into Run-off: the Formation of Equitas to Run-off Certain Lloyd's of London's Liabilities

2.4.1 Lloyd's of London experience

Lloyd's is a market, not a company. It is a leading market for commercial insurance and reinsurance and for personal insurances. It provides a unique concentration of specialist underwriting expertise.

Lloyd's is a very sizeable market. At present, the Lloyd's insurance market has a total capacity to accept insurance premiums of £10 billion. In 1999, 139 syndicates were underwriting insurance at Lloyd's, covering all classes of business from more than one hundred countries world-wide. As outlined above, the presentation of results differs from that conventionally adopted by other insurance organisations. The syndicate underwriting accounts are prepared using the three-year accounting method whereby they are held open for a minimum of 3 years from the commencement of each underwriting year. At the end off the three-year period the accounts are closed by reinsuring outstanding liabilities to the successor syndicate.

2.4.1.1 Lloyd's development

Over the years, Lloyd's reputation was built upon the fact that it never failed to honour a valid claim. From its early beginnings as a Coffee House operated by Edward Lloyd in 1688, Lloyd's developed as a major insurance and reinsurance market over the following 300 years. Its capital structure is somewhat different to a normal insurance/reinsurance company in that, until recently, individuals

(xvii) Many of the policies (even the London ones)are based on an early variant of the claims made form, and most that are not, contain broad tobacco exclusions. Moreover, the industry's largest exposure (the State Attorney's General litigation, the subject of a $206 billion settlement) was couched in terms of restitution, an element of damages not generally recoverable under liability policies.

(known as 'Names') provided the capital to underwrite risks. Whilst there were certain tax advantages to the Names arising from this structure, there was also a large disadvantage – liability was unlimited. Unfortunately, from 1988 – 1992 Lloyd's made a loss in every single year. In five years it lost a total of £7.9 billion. In 1990 alone, the loss was £2.3 billion. These losses were caused in part by the LMX[xviii] Spiral[xix], the reporting of latent claims, and large natural catastrophes. This had a disastrous effect on a number of Names who were faced with large bills. In short, the huge losses and uncertainty over future liabilities endangered the market's existence.

2.4.2 Equitas

2.4.2.1 Why Equitas was formed?

The function of Equitas is to efficiently run-off the business of the syndicates written in the 1992 and previous underwriting years and to eventually return some money to the Names. The company acts in the capacity of run-off agent, and as assignee of the benefit of the reinsurance proceeds. There are two basic reasons why Equitas was formed:

- to allow the individual Names which provided the financial backing to the Lloyd's syndicates to **conclude** their financial affairs by paying in effect, a reinsurance premium to a company that would take over responsibility for running the 1992 and earlier syndicates (other than life syndicates);
- to establish a more **efficient vehicle** for running-off a very large number of syndicates encompassing economies of scale and consistent claims handling issues.;

The stated objectives of Equitas are to endeavour to secure true **finality** for Reinsured Names and in time, to endeavour to create sufficient surplus to enable some return of premium to be made to Reinsured Names. In essence a pot of money has been collected to pay off the known and unknown liabilities of the various syndicates.

(xviii) LMX is an abbreviation for London Market Excess of Loss business

(xix) A so-called spiral effect occurs when excess of loss Reinsurers extensively underwrite each other's excess of loss protections. This leads to a transfer of exposures to the same players within the market rather than their dispersal outside the market.

2.4.2.2 The Structure of Equitas

Equitas received its authority to start operations on 3 September 1996 from the UK Secretary of State. Its original size can be ascertained from its Reports and Accounts as at 31 March 1997:

- it received a premium of £ 11.2 billion, drawn mainly from the Names' Premium Trust Fund (the number of Names involved was in excess of 34,000), but additionally from Lloyd's Central Fund and various other sources;
- it reinsured some 740 Lloyd's syndicate years, in respect of 390 syndicates;
- it had provisions for net claims outstanding of £8.7 billion. More than 40% related to long-tail claims resulting from Asbestos, Pollution and Health Hazard (APH) exposures;
- it had more than 248,500 outwards reinsurance policies with approximately 2,900 Reinsurers. Excess of loss contracts form the vast bulk of active reinsurances that Equitas has had to service;
- it had approximately 1400 members of staff/sub-contractors.

Equitas, as agent for the Names, has wide powers to operate the run-off of the business including claims adjusting and settlement; commutation and set-off; dealing with Reinsurers; and initiation and settlement of litigation.

2.4.2.3 The advantages of Equitas' size and expertise

Equitas has developed professionalism in run-off – by focusing on run-off and commanding the resources to attract the best staff and the ability to invest in the best information technology, Equitas has become one of the leaders in the field of run-off. This is not just in terms of its size but in terms of the methods and working practices it employs. For example, it has introduced 'materiality projects' which aim to attack low value, high cost processes[xx] and it has aggressively commuted parts of its portfolio. Its huge liabilities provide it with access to unrivalled claims information. The Lloyd's syndicates for which Equitas is responsible now have a single voice. This is

(xx) They introduced reinsurance claim collecting note thresholds of $25,000 which immediately removed 56% of their outward reinsurance claims processing whilst delaying recovery of only 7% of their receivables; and they have placed a large number of syndicates into what they term "cold storage" – for these syndicates where the reinsurance asset is small; processing is carried out just once per year.

advantageous for its counterparties who can now deal solely with Equitas rather than a large number of different syndicates.

There is a concentration of power – Equitas is one of the world's largest Reinsurers. Due to its sheer size, Equitas is now an important voice in the industry. It is able to receive a higher rate of interest on its deposits due to the amounts involved and the longer-term over which it is able to invest (syndicates were restricted with respect to the time period over which they could invest). In addition, economies of scale can be achieved leading to a reduction in administration costs.

So far, it has achieved a great deal in a short space of time, although there is a considerable way to go, especially with regard to its asbestos-related exposures. The next several years will be crucial in determining just how much Equitas can accomplish, and indeed, the ultimate success of the project.

CHAPTER 3: DEVELOPING A STRATEGY FOR DISCONTINUED BUSINESS

The ideal is to design a solution which achieves finality over a short period of time and at a low cost, avoiding adverse claims deterioration, so that capital is released to shareholders in a way which is fair to both shareholders and policyholders.

3.1 Introduction

A Company that decides to cease underwriting can, to a large extent, control its own destiny by planning its own strategy for dealing with discontinued business. Such strategic planning sets a direction for an organisation's future success, or alternatively maximises efficiency and minimises costs leaving the company in an optimal position for all stakeholders.

Once a decision to discontinue writing new (or renewal) business has been taken, one of the options is to enter into formal run-off. However, run-off is only one method of several possible methods of ending/transferring the liability, although it is easily the most common, taking place in an estimated 90% of all cases. In this chapter, we will examine how a company can formulate an **optimal discontinued business strategy**.

3.2 Compiling a Strategy for Discontinued Business

Procedurally, the development of a **discontinued business strategy** usually follows five stages:

- defining the **goals** of the company, that is, the business purpose;
- **analysing** the problem areas (for example, quantification of the problem and analysis of the available data);
- **designing** the strategy;
- **implementing** the strategy; and
- **reviewing** the strategy once it is implemented.

What matters is having a forward plan, against which it is possible to **monitor one's progress**. This way, it is possible to judge whether one is on track or not. If not, then remedial action can be implemented before it is too late.

The planning steps required at each stage of the development of a discontinued business strategy can be summarised in the form of a table as follows:

Stage of development	Planning step required
(a) defining goals	1 proposing a change
(b) analyse	2 collecting relevant information
	3 analysing the information and projecting past and present conditions into the future
(c) design	4 designing a set of alternative plans for making the change
	5 selecting the best plan
(d) implementation	6 implementing the selected plan
(e) review	7 monitoring and reviewing the implementation stage
	8 making necessary modifications based on stage 7

Table 8 – The planning steps required at each stage of the development of a discontinued business strategy.

3.3 Goals – Stage 1

3.3.1 The goal of run-off

Upon going into run-off the focus of the organisation changes. The changes may include some of the following (the first nine of these are key and a duplication of those set out in section 2.31. They are included here for the sake of completeness):

Company in run-off	Ongoing company
Main goal: FINALITY i.e. return capital to shareholders and avoid insolvency at all costs	*Main goal: make a profit and increase long-term shareholder value.*
Emphasis on claims	*Emphasis on underwriting*
Main operational purpose: to collect reinsurance claims and distribute funds to policyholders	*Main operational purpose: to underwrite new insurance/reinsurance business*
Major asset is often potential reinsurance recoveries	*Major asset is capital*
Focus on reinsurance recoveries, expense control, cashflow, investment control	*Focus on premium income, market share, new business opportunities*

Legal points often taken on terms and conditions of policies insured/reinsured (leading to savings on inward claims)	*Legal points often* **not** *taken on terms and conditions of policies for commercial reasons*
Staff skills required relate to processing business (especially claims); managing liabilities; and negotiating commutations	*Staff skills required relate to competing for new business by monitoring service levels and innovation*
In theory at least, creditors (i.e. policyholders) interests are paramount due to the scrutiny of the FSA.	*Shareholders interests are paramount*
Views of **FSA** *very important*	*Views of* **FSA** *of less significance although still of importance*
Management seeks to get to grips with the balances due to and from individual entities (that is policyholders/reinsurers often referred to as "Counterparties")	*Management views the inwards claims in terms of different classes of business*
Staff motivation based on a job well done. Long-term employment prospects are limited. In a declining company more individualistic personalities are attracted. Large salaries and staff development programmes used as motivators.	*Staff motivation based on the long-term prospects of a growing company and perceived long term security of employment and promotion*
Cost control by reducing staff; technology; and offices.	*Lean efficiency based on benchmarking*
Increased strain on cash-flow – virtually no premiums, delayed reinsurance recoveries	*Positive cash-flow: income from premiums/reinsurance recoveries/investments*
Annual fluctuation in claims notified can undermine solvency margins	*Annual variability in its liabilities and potential for deterioration in a single year is less critical so long as claims can continue to be paid from current income.*
Net accounting *on it's own is inappropriate.* Principal to principal accounting *(that is, ledgers maintained per policyholder/reinsurer, as well as per broker) often used as a support.*	*Operates on the basis of* net accounting *(that is ledgers simply maintained per broker without a breakdown by policyholder/reinsurer)*
Capital is limited (i.e. restricted)	*Capital is generally adequate, and there is a wide scope for capital injection.*
Primary function of inwards broker is to promptly advise claim settlements and reserves. Primary function of outwards broker is the rapid collection and remittance of reinsurance recoveries. Broker sometimes paid extra fee to collect outward claims	*Primary function of inwards broker is to produce profitable business. Primary function of outwards broker is the placement of outward reinsurance protections with quality security, and to service the contracts. Broker fee for claims collection included in brokerage*

(continued overleaf)

Computer system requirements geared to control of claims costs and cash flow. Improvements may be required in the claims, credit control, and retrocession areas.	*Computer system requirements geared to improved underwriting decisions, and monitoring of aggregate exposures.*
Company feels it is not part of the market, and acts accordingly. For example, it may cease to be a member of a central settlement system since this slows down inward claim payments. It only feels part of the market to the extent that it has to collect reinsurance claims. It's interests are best served by reviewing its own selfish requirements.	*Company feels it is a part of the market, and acts to maintain service levels and competitiveness.*

Table 9 – Change in strategy when a company enters run-off.

Where run-off is chosen as the strategy, the main goal is likely to be financial finality. For the run-off owner, finality is the expiration or extinguishment of liabilities. Once such liabilities are at an end, the residual capital, if any, is returned to the shareholders.

Subsidiary run-off aims centre on achieving:

- **a short period of run-off** – an approach that is likely to shorten the run-off period. Evidence of this approach can be seen at Equitas where, despite the fact that the majority of their remaining portfolio is long-tail liability business, the vision exists to shorten the development tail at every turn and their business plan is aimed at achieving this goal;
- **increase income** (i.e. invest wisely – in contrast to the above, the longer the investment period the higher the return on fixed interest investments; critically, the stream of investment income must be matched to the expected payout pattern and currency of the reserved claims.);
- **decrease expenses** (i.e. cost reductions – the major expenses are staff; office; and technology. However, there is an inherent conflict here since high quality staff and systems are required.);
- **increase assets** (i.e. process and collect reinsurance recoveries efficiently/promptly and possibly commute with Reinsurers, at a time to suit);
- **decrease liabilities** (i.e. pay only valid claims and commute with policyholders – these are your creditors).

In practical terms, the aims require:

(a) centralised credit control – i.e. identify all recoveries due from one party (known as "principal to principal accounting");

(b) control of cash-flow (it should be noted that an inability to meet claims as they fall due is insolvency under the Insolvency Act 1986);

(c) commuting pro-actively according to a predetermined commutation strategy (explained later in this book);

(d) management of claims in accordance with a predetermined philosophy;

(e) compliance with statutory company reporting requirements;

(f) being equitable with policyholders;

(g) maintenance of goodwill with Cedants, Reinsurers, and Brokers i.e. avoid long-term damage to market reputation (this is especially applicable where a portion of the company or group remains in the ongoing market).

It should be noted that goals are not set in stone. If a run-off company is successful in its chosen strategy e.g. aggressive commutation, then its prospects may change (e.g. its solvency may increase) and a review of strategy may reveal that new goals now take priority.

3.3.2 The different stakeholders in an insurance/reinsurance organisation

Up to now we have talked about goals as if there was only one group in whose interests the company is run – the shareholders.

There are in fact several 'stakeholders' in an insurance/reinsurance organisation including:

- shareholders;
- policyholders;
- employees and contract workers;
- management;
- brokers;
- the Regulator.

David, F.R. (1993)[i] defines stakeholders as

> *"the individuals and groups of persons who have a special stake or claim on the company" (p. 98)*

This definition is very imprecise since there is no priority of interests. It is exactly this setting of priorities which is at the crux of the problem. As David, F. R. continues:

> *"All stakeholders' claims on an organisation cannot be pursued with equal emphasis"*

3.3.3 Prioritisation of stakeholders

As outlined in the table above (see Table 8), upon going into run-off the focus of the organisation changes. One of these changes relates to the prioritisation of stakeholders. For a company in run-off, in theory at least, creditors' (i.e. policyholders') interests are paramount as a consequence of the scrutiny of the FSA who regulate such companies. The FSA, on behalf of the UK government seeks to protcct policyholders by ensuring that Insurers and Reinsurers are able to pay claims when they arise.

This compares with ongoing companies where shareholders interests are paramount.

The role of the Regulator is discussed in greater detail later in this book.

3.3.4 Goals of the policyholders

The goals of the policyholders upon the announcement of run-off relate essentially to the fact that the company **remains solvent** and therefore able to meet their claims as and when they fall due for payment. Given that the policyholder has entered into a legally binding contract with the (Re)Insurer and has paid a premium in return for the promise to be reimbursed in the event of a claim, the financial strength of the Insurer/Reinsurer is vital. This is especially important in the case of reinsurance policies where latent claims (such as asbestos-related claims) can continue to be reported many years after the policy period (in some cases up to 40 years later) – this is referred to as long-tail business. In addition, even 'known' claims (i.e. those which have already been reported to the insurance/reinsurance company) can take

---

(i) David F R (1993) *Concepts of Strategic Management* Macmillan publishing Co. New York

many years to settle. All this means that the insurance/reinsurance company may be called to make good its original promise many years after having received the premium. Whether the company in run-off has adequately reinsured itself with financially secure Reinsurers will obviously play a role in the solvency of the company in run-off.

Secondary considerations relate to the fact that the run-off will be conducted in an orderly and efficient manner and that every effort is made to ensure that all aspects of the company's administration are maintained to the highest standard and in particular, that **all valid claims are paid promptly**. In this context, it is important to note whether the company's parent company, if applicable, is fully committed to ensuring that the legitimate claims of the company's policyholders are honoured in full, and the extent of the financial resources of the parent company. (As noted earlier, each company within a group of companies is a separate legal entity with limited liability. The parent company, for example, is not legally liable for the debts of its subsidiaries unless it has agreed to assume responsibility for them or there are other special circumstances. Such financial 'commitment' would therefore relate to a commercial decision to retain the goodwill of its customers).

It should also be noted that there might well be more than one group of policyholders, each with their own differing interests, as follows:

- policyholders with short-tail liabilities – they seek settlement of their claims within for example 3 to 5 years. If the run-off becomes insolvent after this time, their individual interests are unaffected;
- policyholders with long-tail liabilities – they seek settlement of their claims within for example 40 years – they therefore have an interest in the long-term financial health of the company in run-off. They may not have claims at present but instead have contingent claims which may manifest themselves in the future. Actuarial estimates are used to predict the ultimate losses. (With any run-off, long-tail policyholders are exposed to a greater risk of bearing run-off costs, as Insurers' cash resources are depleted over time, with the risk that assets will be exhausted before liabilities).

It is the existence of this second group of policyholders which makes the designing of run-off solutions so difficult as the potential claim amount is uncertain and therefore difficult to accurately budget for.

3.3.5 The goals of Employees; Management; Brokers; Regulator; Reinsurer; Guarantor; and Third Party run-off Manager.

The goals of each of these parties is often that shown below:

- employees/contract workers – seeking continuing employment;
- management – seeking continuing employment at an executive level;
- brokers – minimising the costs and problems of non-current business;
- regulator – protecting policyholders' interests and regulating solvency;
- reinsurer – minimise claims payments and maximise claims recoveries from its own Reinsurers and retrocessionaires;
- guarantor – minimise calls on guarantees and avoid long-term damage to market reputation;
- third party run-off manager – seeking continuing employment.

As can be seen from the above analysis, there are a variety of different goals being pursued. Each stakeholder will have its own goal and an associated strategy. For example, if management and run-off managers seek to continue their employment they may try (even subconsciously) to prolong the run-off (or at least not try to end the run-off too soon)[ii]. Shareholders, on the other hand, want the reverse: the shortest practicable run-off and a prompt realisation of their investment.

This is the classic problem when considering the differing interests of the stakeholders as there is a conflict between the interests of one group *vis-à-vis* another.

3.4 Analyse – Stage 2

In order to make an informed decision regarding the most appropriate discontinued business strategy the management requires detailed information. The analysis stage can be broken down into two distinct phases:

(ii) This problem is exasperated where the run-off is handled by a third party administrator who is remunerated on the basis of transactions processed rather than the success in achieving finality within a given timeframe. Obviously there is vested interest in keeping the run-off going as long as possible to generate fee income.

- collecting relevant information;
- analysing the information and projecting past and present conditions into the future.

Such analysis will enable a logical decision to be made regarding the optimum route to be taken to extinguish all liability and obligations.

3.4.1 collecting relevant information

There are three areas, which need to be researched, as follows:

- liabilities;
- assets;
- run-off costs, including staff and IT resources.

3.4.1.1 Liabilities

Whilst the management is likely to have management reports at its disposal, it is necessary to evaluate the portfolio in-depth in order to analyse what lies behind the management reports. Whilst to an untrained eye a portfolio may appear to be non-hazardous in respect of the liabilities it contains, to an expert a brief review of the key cedants and well-known problem contracts will alert him to the fact that this portfolio is potentially a timebomb. In such a situation reinsurance consultants and claim experts might be used to skilfully ascertain the extent of the liabilities. Their objective is to facilitate a clear and objective view of the insurance/reinsurance liabilities, with particular emphasis on the source of exposure to further claims by policy type. To determine the real exposure the following areas should be analysed:

- identify key contracts – the portfolio will by definition, be made up of a myriad of different contracts. The key to ascertaining the exposure is to identify those contracts that contain the bulk of the problem areas, which will make or break the discontinued business strategy. The length of period a company remains on risk after cessation of underwriting can be longer than expected. Line slips, multi-year policies and extended discovery periods on claims-made policies all extend the period on risk. A key contract is characterised by:

    (a) a contract which has the potential to respond to latent claims, especially those emanating from the US (such as asbestos-related and pollution claims) i.e. liability policies;

(b) large outstanding losses;

(c) large historical premium income;

(d) unlimited reinstatements;

(e) large paid claims in relation to the premium received and unexhausted cover;

(f) contracts which are the subject of litigation or arbitration between the company and the policyholder;

(g) heavy administration burden e.g. contracts with a high frequency of losses and a "costs in addition" clause; an index clause; or a currency clause.

- identify the key policyholders – this aspect needs to be considered in association with the key contracts identification above. Certain policyholders may be very exposed to problematical liabilities (such as asbestos-related and pollution claims). Hence any Reinsurer of such policyholders will likewise be hit with these exposures sooner or later. Other policyholders attempt to collect claims that are somewhat doubtful; others may be very litigious or difficult to negotiate with. Some policyholders may be in liquidation and again these contracts require special attention. Policyholders that are financially insecure may not have recovered reinsurance claims for some time – hence a large number of claims may be in the pipeline. Factors to consider are:

  (a) the number of reported claims;

  (b) the size of the IBNR[iii] reserves;

  (c) possible time bar[iv] defences;

(iii) Incurred but not reported reserve ("IBNR" reserve) -This reserve covers claims that have been incurred but not yet reported to the company. This reserve is calculated by using statistical techniques based upon the Insurer's past experience of claims and various other information, such as legislation, market knowledge and judicial developments.

(iv) Once a cause of action has accrued to a party a limitation period (e.g. 6 years)is laid down by statute (or contract) within which legal proceedings must be commenced. Failure to bring proceedings does not deprive potential claimants (i.e. plaintiffs) of their cause of action. The defendant will however be able to prevent it continuing on the basis that it has been brought outside the relevant limitation period. This is known as being "time-barred".

(d) possible standstill[v] agreements in place with the policyholders.

- assess data quality – the data held by the Reinsurer may be of questionable quality (e.g. data is held on computer but cannot be evidenced by physical documentation; or the data held is incomplete with contractual terms unknown or incorrectly recorded on computer; alternatively, the Broker holds the majority of the information and is unable or unwilling to provide the details). This is a common problem in cases where the contracts relate to reinsurance contracts dating back over a number of years. Whilst files are unlikely to be fully complete, there may come a point when the quality of data will severely affect the reliability that can be placed on any analysis undertaken. (In such a situation, the development of a commutation strategy is perhaps a practical solution as discussed later in this book). A company, which has this problem, may have their accounts qualified by the auditors.
- assess past internal claims procedures – different attitudes of insurance/reinsurance companies towards claims reserving provide one example of why further analysis may be needed to obtain useful management information. For example, varying options regarding liability for pollution claims will be reflected in differing reserve levels. The exposure can be hidden if nominal precautionary reserves are established, since the amounts posted are below the threshold for executive or head office review. In addition, standards adopted by the (Re)Insurer to manage the claims, especially latent claims, and the use of a written claims philosophy[vi] (and whether it was adhered to in practice) can have a dramatic effect on the company's future exposure under the contracts. (In legal terms, the company may have affirmed the contract – in brief, confirmed its existence – and waived its rights depending upon the actual circumstances and actions undertaken).

The greatest uncertainty in reserves is, of course, the estimation of IBNR reserves. No matter how basic or sophisticated the process, there is inevitably a range of possible outcomes and the range may be substantial. The estimate that a company's management selects within the range (each period) contributes to the unrecognised exposure. It is

---

(v) A standstill is essentially an agreement signed by both parties not to apply time bar defences (either indefinitely or for a stated period). In effect 'time stands still' since the time within which the potential claimant (i.e. plaintiff) must commence the proceedings stops running.

(vi) For a discussion on the use of written claims philosophies refer to Peter Wedge – Chartered Insurance Institute Textbook – *Claims Management* May 2000.

self-evident that a company that always selects a point at the low end of the range of ultimate outcomes is more likely to be exposed to future deterioration in the event that unexpected claims arise.

3.4.1.2 Assets

Parallel with an examination of the underlying contractual situation, it is also appropriate to determine which assets are available to the company in terms of fixed assets (such as buildings); existing financial instruments; investments; and capital. Key employees can also be regarded as assets. As such, these should also be identified and contractually tied in to the company (perhaps by offering termination bonuses).

For a company in run-off, reinsurance assets will include reinsurance recoveries, premiums, surplus on Letters of Credit (i.e. the amount in excess of the current outstanding loss reserve), unearned premium reserves and any funds being held by others in the advent of a claim, e.g. managing agents or brokers.

3.4.1.3 Run-off costs (e.g. staff and IT resources)

Whether or not an organisation chooses the run-off solution to deal with its retrospective liabilities after ceasing to underwrite business, the administration costs of such a run-off must be calculated in order to work out benchmark costs for alternatives[vii]. The key costs are staff; IT; and premises. With respect to staff, the number and skills required must be ascertained. The skills of the management are critical in this regard. In many cases long-term contracts are entered into with IT suppliers and /or landlords and the precise details of any penalty clauses must be made available and understood in this information gathering stage.

It is necessary to analyse the run-off cost over the hypothetical run-off period (sometimes taken to be a hypothetical 5 years or 10 years).

3.4.2 analysing the information and projecting past and present conditions into the future

Once the required information has been gathered it can then be analysed in an intelligent manner in order to comprehend its

(vii) The opportunity costs are those costs which would have arose had an alternative course of action been chosen. They provide a basis for comparison for the actual course of action chosen.

significance. In essence raw data is transformed into information (i.e. data presented in such a way that it enables decisions to be made). Judgements are needed by experienced practitioners on possible future claims development, levels of current and future bad debts, outcome of litigation and run-off costs.

It also involves understanding the company's internal capabilities to identify strengths and weaknesses in each of the areas in question and assessing the threats and opportunities from the external environment.

In terms of each of the above areas, the following should be undertaken:

3.4.2.1 Liabilities

Once liabilities are identified, quantification of the "end-of-the-day" ultimate liabilities is required (in simple terms this is an estimate of the maximum claims payable). There are broadly two methods to be applied: Firstly, the key contracts need to be assessed either internally by claims experts or externally using reinsurance consultants (who are specialists in claims audits) following a bottom up approach i.e. are case loss reserves adequate on a per claim file basis? The contracts should be graded as to severity (i.e. their theoretical propensity to respond to long-tail liabilities[viii]) and priority of action. In addition, it should be ensured that contracts noted as 'commuted' are finally closed (i.e. they cannot be subsequently re-opened). Secondly, are overall loss reserves adequate (including IBNR)? It is important to engage external actuarial and financial input in addition to internal resources to ensure independent opinions. The actuaries should project expected ultimate loss and loss adjustment expenses and then subject those projections to a number of different "stress" scenarios with the goal of determining the probability of the various outcomes. Gross results (before application of reinsurance) and net results should also be projected and the recoverability of losses which will be collected from Reinsurers needs to be quantified. Finally, expected payouts of losses under each scenario will be required to measure the present value of the liabilities.[ix]

(viii) Legal assistance may be needed on larger contracts where the legal liability may be uncertain and the potential liability very large.

(ix) Where the run-off option is chosen as the solution, the Financial Services Authority will expect to see a five year plan with an actuarial review of the liabilities which encompasses a realistic assessment of claims.

3.4.2.2 Assets

Principal among these must be a company's reinsurance programme. It is vital to analyse the amount of reinsurance protection that remains unused and the bad debt write-down applicable to the asset. This will in turn depend upon the financial quality and integrity of the Reinsurers on the programme. In addition, certain Reinsurers (who may also act as cedants, which is frequent in the reinsurance market) may be more amenable to the prospect of a commutation than others. The type of reinsurance cover in place and the attitude of the Reinsurers to paying settlements that have been compromised at the insurance level are also important here. It is essential to get the Reinsurers on side if the run-off is to be completed successfully and solvently.

The results of these quantifications will determine the amount of capital that needs to be allocated to support the operation. In addition, supplemental sources of capital should be structured (such as reinsurance or lines of credit) to ensure that the new entity will be self-sustaining and will not require future capital injections from the parent company.

3.4.2.3 Run-off costs

The administration cost of a run-off is difficult to assess but is estimated to be about 20% of gross liabilities[x]. The biggest unknown is the **time** involved to run-off the contingent liabilities.

It requires detailed assessment of the company's operation. This entails a preliminary visit to the appropriate offices by a small, experienced team of claim experts or reinsurance consultants. The team could examine the records and staff on-site and prepare a formal proposal as to how the run-off could be conducted, the systems and methodology to be applied and a rough estimate of time and cost scale involved.

As outlined earlier in this book, it should be noted that different management skills are required to handle a company in run-off to those needed to manage the operations of an active insurance or reinsurance company. It must be determined which individuals are able to carry out the work efficiently, and are indeed sufficiently motivated and able to administer the portfolio.

(x) PricewaterhouseCoopers – *The managed exits of the future – how to save US$50 billion* November 1999.

Such an analysis would provide the (Re)Insurer with a much better understanding of the portfolio.

3.5 Design – Stage 3

Legally, an insurance/reinsurance company, run-off or otherwise, cannot be dissolved if it is solvent and there are still potential claims to come in – it must therefore design a solution to the problem of the continuing liabilities.

The ideal is to design a solution which:

- **achieves finality;**
- **over a short time;**
- **at a low cost;**
- **to avoid adverse claims deterioration;**
- **so that capital is released to shareholders in a way which is fair to both shareholders and policyholders.**

The current options for a discontinued business strategy can be categorised as being either:

- insurance based or
- non-insurance based.

Ideally, all available options should be considered by senior management (and the company's shareholders) in order to determine the exit route best suited to the circumstances of the company.

Listed below are the current solutions highlighting both their advantages and disadvantages. Not all are available to every company, depending, *inter alia*, upon the exact circumstances surrounding the reasons for the company ceasing to write business; and the nature of the portfolio under consideration. Unfortunately there is no universal solution to the problem of discontinued business.

3.5.1 Insurance solutions

3.5.1.1 Ignore the problem of continuing bad underwriting results

Where underwriting results deteriorate suddenly, it is possible that the company may just be going through a bad patch, viewed in the context of the wider market. The initial and correct action may be to weather the storm and to cope with what is hopefully a temporary problem, which will remain under control. During this period there is a dependence upon current income to pay claims. It is interesting to note that up until the mid-1980's (when premium rates were historically low and hence income streams were depleted) most companies faced with retrospective liabilities chose to handle them internally by ignoring them or by managing them within the stream of normal business.

If bad underwriting results persist, the company may decide to increase rates and control expenses. If these measures have limited effect, tough decisions will have to be made regarding the future viability of the operation (or part thereof). The point at which a company decides to stop underwriting will depend, *inter alia*, in rough order of priority, upon:

- the attitude of the funding provider e.g. shareholders or the parent company;
- the state of the market in general and future prospects of returning to profit;
- the financial resources available;
- the attitude of the management;
- the scale of the losses;
- the attitude of the regulator.

The more detailed the management's knowledge of their portfolio, the less the danger of not recognising the seriousness of any financial problems which might arise. There is therefore an advantage to be gained from regular reviews of the portfolio by internal or external experts to ensure that information systems and procedures are working smoothly.

The disadvantage of ignoring the problem of continuing bad underwriting results is that for many Insurers the problem will not go away and will become more difficult, if not impossible, to resolve in the future. Such Insurers – if they survive – often become vulnerable to acquisition.

As was experienced recently in the case of Australian Reinsurers New Cap Re and GIO, in cases where a company is hit by sudden devastating claims payments the option of the company putting its head into the sand does not exist.

3.5.1.2 Run-off

This option rests on the strategy that business lines may be run-off until all claims have been paid. As noted above this option is selected in roughly 90% of all cases.

Where an entity in run-off is part of group of companies an appropriate run-off strategy must deal with the following issues:

1. Risk to equity :
   - inefficient use of capital – the modern business world is characterised by sophisticated investors and well-developed capital markets. Making effective use of capital is one of the most significant problems faced by senior management. Industry commentators believe that much of the capital employed in discontinued business is not earning its opportunity cost; that is the returns available by investing these funds elsewhere;
   - block on extraction of shareholder value – until the run-off can be closed, shareholders are unable to extract the value of shareholder equity.
2. Risk to profitability:
   - deterioration of claims and reinsurance – there is a risk that claims will worsen over the lifetime of the run-off and that Reinsurers will become insolvent and/or reinsurance protections be exhausted. These are discussed further below;
   - the administration costs of protracted run-off – such costs can prove to be material, as outlined below;
   - volatility of investment earnings – the main source of income for a run-off is investment income. Hence any volatility in interest rates and other types of investment may require the parent to provide a capital injection.
3. Risk to management of business:
   - diversion of senior management – rather than focus on on-going business, senior management is side-tracked into dealing with complicated, often non-profit making issues concerning the run-off operation;
   - non-core activity – for many organisations the run-off industry is something which they have stumbled into and it is not considered a core activity of the group as a whole;

- exposure to parental financial guarantees – financial guarantees are often provided to entities in run-off due to their history of requiring more capital over the course of the run-off. Unfortunately, such guarantees have a habit of being called upon.

4. Risk to reputation:

- financial performance below industry benchmarks;
- failure of company in run-off to meet claims – in the event that the run-off entity is unable to meet its claims, despite it being a separate legal entity, the reputation of the group as a whole is bound to suffer.

We can distinguish between two types of run-off, as follows:

3.5.1.2.1 Passive Run-off

Passive run-off can be defined as:

> "Conducting the run-off without any apparent goal of finality; a lack of concern over the length of the run-off ; and not taking into account the total costs of the run-off over its whole lifetime. There is a focus upon expense minimisation and mitigating only major/problem losses. In short, the run-off is conducted in a similar fashion to that of an on-going portfolio".

In many cases, companies which form part of a group, where other companies within the group have on-going live operations, adopt this approach.

The archetypal[xi] passive run-off company:

- takes a passive stance on commutations. It sets commutation priorities based upon low value, high volume treaties;
- does not maintain an active IT diary system for reinsurance claim recovery;
- follows the Lead Underwriter in claims decisions as a matter of course; and
- to shareholders, management and staff its goal is unknown and its future uncertain.

(xi) Adapted from *Why is there not an end to run-off?* Leslie Ann Giovnilli.

Lack of leadership means adopting a passive approach by default.

The **advantages** of adopting a passive run-off approach include:

- employment opportunities are retained for staff if the run-off is kept in-house and not outsourced. This avoids making sensitive decisions in the short-term;
- in the short-term it is a simple option since there is very little difference to an on-going company;
- in the short-term the approach will avoid damage to market reputation;
- in the short-term, expenses are kept to a minimum;
- the approach therefore appeals to groups who have live operations which remain in the insurance/reinsurance market.

The **disadvantages** include:

- running-off discontinued business may not be a core activity for the company (since in many cases the company was, until recently, an active Underwriter). Therefore the myriad of specialist run-off skills is not available to the company. Indeed the run-off is often conducted without a clear run-off strategy. Given the history of companies in run-off, without a clear strategy insolvency is a distinct possibility. Lack of interest by senior management often leads to problems since strong decisions are required to be made;
- the risk that the run-off is forgotten about and then noticed when it goes wrong;
- in the long-term, financial problems may arise because:

  (a) run-off to expiry takes a long time and costs do not fall as quickly as liabilities – historically run-off to expiry is rarely achieved. Almost every company has entered some sort of scheme of arrangement (whether an insolvent scheme or solvent scheme) or become insolvent. There is in effect a race between assets and liabilities to see what will expire first. This problem is reinforced in the current low interest environment, where investment income is lower and may fall below that needed to finance the annual run-off costs;

  (b) over time, costs tend to increase relative to liabilities due to fixed costs which are now spread over a smaller portfolio and unforeseen adverse claims development (which often requires more claims handling resource). A passive run-off favours the interests of policyholders with short-term liabilities.

3.5.1.2.2 Pro-active run-off

Pro-active run-off can be defined as

> "Conducting the run-off with an openly stated goal of finality; minimising and mitigating losses to the maximum extent possible and shortening the life of the run-off via the use of such tools as commutation and inspections of records."[xii]

There is a tacit recognition of the long-term value added by the use of external experts[xiii] skilled in the art of run-off. In short, the run-off is conducted on a completely different footing to that of an on-going company in terms of the methods and working practices it employs.

The archetypal pro-active run-off company:

- concentrates resources upon a dynamic commutation strategy (defined below) utilising its best staff and information technology towards this end. (However, some portfolios require to be managed for investment to remain solvent and can only commute on a selective basis);
- adopts a strict approach to claims payment based upon the legal parameters of the contract;
- identifies cases where internal or external resources should be utilised to conduct inspections of records;
- focuses upon active reinsurance claim recovery;
- its goal is clear to shareholders, management and staff alike.

A pro-active approach will involve the investment of resources in

- actively seeking to monitor and control the loss development (with funds spent on auditing or claims control being compared to the benefits derived through savings in loss values).
- increased attention to credit control (enabling a comparison to be made between the increased cost of staff and the improved cash flow/investment income).

(xii) An inspection of records involves the Reinsurer inspecting the books and records of the insurer on-site. Often the main concern is the validity of the reinsurance claims presented and the associated issues of underwriting guidelines and representations made. For more on inspections of records generally see ARC's *Manual on Inspections of Records* edited by Peter Wedge.

(xiii) See *Run-Off Management in Practice*, Ivor Kiverstein, Chiltington website – (www.chiltington.co.uk)

Within this spectrum, some companies would regard inspection of records as a tool of last resort and concentrate on strict claims handling with informed claims management. They combine this with close investment and cash flow monitoring.

It should be noted that there is a fine line between conducting a run-off on a pro active basis and conducting it on an aggressive basis. The latter is characterised by the creation of strategic delays through 'creative' disputes and deliberately slowing claims payment for no valid reason. The maxim adopted by aggressive run-off companies appears to be "make a mountain out of a molehill". Claims managers become litigating aggressors who refute liability wherever possible. Such companies give the professionals a bad name and attempt to make a nuisance of themselves at every turn. Fortunately, the insurance/reinsurance industry is a small community and companies acting in bad faith will not prosper long-term. Indeed, if an aggressive run-off strategy makes it difficult for policyholders to be paid claims in full on due dates the regulator may be concerned.

In contrast, pro-active companies use such tools as inspections of records in a productive and professional manner, concentrating upon those issues which go to the heart of the relationship and which can truly be considered significant. They seek to restrict the payment of claims to those, which are properly due under the terms of the contract rather than avoiding their liabilities.

To the extent that it achieves an earlier end to the liabilities, the **advantages** of adopting a pro-active approach may include:

- the minimisation of uncertainty – there is uncertainty inherent in the length of the run-off and the ultimate claims costs[xiv]. In particular, the ultimate claims costs of long-term liabilities such as Asbestos, Pollution, and other Health Hazard risks are subject to material uncertainty[xv]. Such liabilities may take up to 50 years to settle. Furthermore, there is a danger of as yet unknown types of loss manifesting themselves;
- the minimisation of the administrative costs associated with run-

---

(xiv) The current discounted value of the insurance industry's environmental liability exposure is estimated at US$ 40 billion to US$50 billion. Source – *USA Superfund fallout*, Reinsurance, May 1999

(xv) Actuaries forecast up to 50 years to conclude some casualty reinsurance claims (e.g. those with toxic tort) according to Global Reinsurance, *Run-off: new strategies for an old business*, Volume 7, Issue 7.

off. These costs can be significant and are estimated to be approximately 20% of gross liabilities;[xvi]

- reduction of the interest rate risk – companies in run-off are heavily dependent upon investment income. If the main investments are in variable interest assets there is a risk that interest rates will fall and the investment income will be insufficient to pay claims and the administration costs of the run-off (which increase with inflation). Furthermore, when interest rates are falling this leads to declining discount rates which in turn has the effect of increasing the level of discounted reserves which are required. With regard to commutations, there is a balance to be found between retaining funds to invest and commuting liabilities to get a discount on the amounts paid;
- reduction of the exposure to adverse claim deterioration. Such deterioration occurs quite often due to the underestimation of long-term liabilities (initial reserves being based upon limited knowledge especially with regard to medical conditions and underlying causes); under-reserving by the insurance/reinsurance company; increased compensation payments due to social inflation and increased amounts of litigation; courts interpreting coverage in ways which were never anticipated; and new causes of loss which tend to appear over the years;
- mitigation of the risk of Reinsurers becoming insolvent and therefore being unable to pay claims in full. In addition, inward claims deterioration may lead to reinsurance protections being exhausted over time. Insurers in run-off may also prefer to commute with Reinsurers and so liquidate potential future reinsurance recoverables so that the reinsurance asset can generate funds to be invested;
- where the entity in run-off is part of a group, an early exit minimises the time that precious capital is tied up in a run-off entity. Run-off operations are not regarded favourably by the wider investment market due to the uncertainty they create so such a company may have adverse affects upon the share price of the group. There is also the opportunity costs of the capital to consider. Furthermore, it frees management to focus upon on-going and new business;

(xvi) PricewaterhouseCoopers – *The managed exits of the future – how to save US$50 billion* November 1999.

- policyholders will be paid quicker than otherwise would have been the case.

The **disadvantages** include:

- the initial set-up costs of the run-off operation on a new footing can be substantial;
- inspections of records and any resulting litigation can be expensive. This is not a problem where fundamental issues are found in the inspection and then litigated, but where arguments are of a more technical nature, the costs need to be closely compared to the economic gain;
- a pro-active stance may not sit comfortably with the culture of the parent organisation. Certainly aggressive run-off is impractical for organisations with operations in the live market – market reputation can be seriously damaged;
- a very pro-active stance may result in retaliatory litigation on other insurance/reinsurance contracts;
- a pro-active stance requires high reinsurance technical skills to be properly implemented – the run-off manager must be able to spot issues on strict claims handling and use inspections of records, arbitration, and litigation only when appropriate. It requires a knowledge of how to present the issues and an ability of knowing when to compromise – in short the ability of making the issues work for you;
- in the event that claims are paid sooner than anticipated there is an acceleration in the claims pay-out pattern which needs to be budgeted for.

Both passive and pro-active run-offs will need a plan with a specified budget for anticipated expenses and projected cash flow.

3.5.1.2.3 Commutations

A *commutation* can be defined as:

> **"an agreement to release the Insurer from all past, present, and future liability under the insurance contract in return for a lump sum cash payment now"**

It is used by insurers and reinsurers alike to bring the liabilities under insurance and reinsurance contracts to an end, changing them from ongoing contracts to crystallised sums of money which will never alter.

Especially at the start of the operation of the run-off, it is best practice to devise a commutation strategy. A *commutation strategy* can be defined as:

"Commuting pro actively according to a predetermined plan."

A plan is required due to the fact that resources are limited and it is not possible to commute with every party at one time. An approach of pro-active commutation takes significant time and resource. It principally requires initiating commutation discussions with Reinsurers; comparing the company's outward reinsurance contracts with those contract details supplied by the Reinsurer; and negotiating commutation deals. Critically, the estimation of the ultimate liabilities can be a lengthy exercise. In all of the above, companies must strive to be as effective as possible for the minimum of effort. This can be achieved by setting priorities to focus resource where it can achieve most. Good management information is needed to follow this maxim closely. Without a clear strategy, a focused approach and good information, high expenses can be incurred for only a limited reward.

An important element in devising such a strategy will be the correct identification of commutation targets, and a prioritisation of such targets. Such plans may target weak Reinsurers first or perhaps the most willing counterparties since these ensure that the commutation actually takes place within a predefined timeframe.

The selection of Reinsurers for commutations may take some or all of the following issues into account:

- the type of business – the more long-tail the exposure the greater the need to commute in general terms;
- solvency of the Reinsurer;
- types of reinsurance contract, for example, excess of loss or quota share;
- the absolute value in cash terms of the commutation – larger commutations may be preferred since they can save a larger amount of run-off administration costs (depending upon circumstances);
- the volatility of the inwards book of business – more volatile accounts will be targeted first due to their effect upon cash flow and processing effort required;

- willingness of the counterparty to commute – a willing counterparty will throw resources at the problem and ensure that hurdles are overcome within a reasonable timeframe. He will treat the commutation as a priority rather than an annoyance;
- resource constraints within the run-off company itself;
- amount of work involved;
- feasibility of carrying out the commutation;
- reliability of data;
- cost/benefit analysis;
- settlement issues; contractual disputes, and credit control delays.

We can distinguish between four types of commutation:

- single claim;
- single contract;
- multi-contract;
- whole relationship, that is every single inwards and outwards contract between the entity in run-off and a certain Reinsurer (this is known as a "global commutation"). A global commutation between two parties may incorporate a large number of reinsurance treaties both ways involving potentially thousands of ledger transactions.

Commutation has long been a traditional tool in the strategy of a *financially strong* company in run-off. The prime objectives are usually:

- poor Reinsurer security – it might be in the company's best interests to commute with such Reinsurers even though the full extent of their liability to the company in run-off is difficult to ascertain;
- reducing inwards exposure – if certainty of result can be achieved by commutation, shareholders will be much more willing to pay the price;
- reducing run-off administration costs – this becomes more and more necessary for run-off companies as the levels of their reserves reduce at a faster rate than their expenses (thus increasing the ratio of expenses to funds under management);
- to achieve finality – commutation is one of the few methods of

achieving finality. There is no come back (so long as the commutation agreement has been properly drafted).

The company's Reinsurers will also be important parts of each deal, and achieving agreement with them will be essential for cash flow because there is no certain method of recovering amounts paid in commutation of outstanding loss reserves and IBNR.[xvii]

Commutation is also a traditional tool where the company in run-off is *financially weak*. Fear will drive policyholders or Cedants to commute and discounts will be obtainable, which will assist the solvency margin. The support of Reinsurers will most likely be crucial to cash flow. As time progresses, sometimes the biggest difficulty is staying solvent as the remaining book gets worse.

Commutations, in various forms, have been carried out for a very long time but it is only in the 1990's that they have become commonplace.

The calculation of the IBNR figure within a commutation deal is usually the most difficult to calculate, since, despite the use of actuaries there is likely to be an element of guesswork in arriving at an acceptable figure for both parties. In addition, both parties may be tempted to inflate their figures to increase their safety margins or to enhance their solvency margins.

To carry out a successful commutation strategy requires superior negotiation and risk assessment skills and excellent communication channels between commutation and reinsurance recovery specialists. Properly executed, it is one of the main ways in which value can be added to a company in run-off. However, there is a balance to be found between retaining funds to invest and commuting liabilities to get a discount on the amounts paid.

3.5.1.3 Cap exposure by conventional reinsurance.

One insurance solution would be to buy conventional reinsurance, either on a stop loss or aggregate excess of loss basis, which effectively places a cap on the exposure by transferring the risk to another party. This would be a form of run-off reinsurance that reinsures the entire portfolio (i.e. all contracts forming the book of business).

There is now a market for the provision of long-tail reinsurance, and carriers are actively seeking business to underwrite.

(xvii) For more on commutations in general and this issue in particular, refer to ARC's *Manual on Commutations* edited by Peter Wedge.

The most commonly offered product is some form of cover against adverse development of long-tail losses (such as asbestos-related, pollution, and health-hazard exposures known as APH exposures. For example, a $50 million limit may be provided over a 10 year period in excess of the Reinsured's existing insurance programme with a large portion of the limit being funded by the reinsurance premium. If the coverage is not fully used during the period, a portion of the premium can be returned to the Reinsured.). Amounts of exposure considered can be as low as $3m to as much as $100m and above

It should be noted that at present very few, if any, carriers would be willing to offer an unlimited reinsurance of the entire book of business. However, some Reinsurers may offer very high limits which are the closest to unlimited coverage that is currently available.

The process itself is essentially straightforward in concept: the reinsurer will evaluate the exposure and quote a premium to underwrite the risk. The underwriting process may involve an initial assessment of the opportunity followed by a brief review of the subject business which may be covered by the transaction. Copies of available relevant documents (such as actuarial studies, annual statements, underwriting submissions and loss runs) will be reviewed by a claims specialist. Following this phase, an indication may be sent to the run-off owner. If he agrees and is interested in the proposed structure, the run-off owner may have to fund a detailed and extremely thorough review of the entire book. This will require a combination of actuarial assessment and input from reinsurance and claims specialists to reach a satisfactory evaluation of the potential exposure. The aim of this review will be to identify trends/issues which could negatively impact the proposed transaction and to quantify those negatives. The claims specialist needs to identify and understand all obligations the run-off owner seeks to be reinsured. The Reinsurer will then prepare a quotation based on the information produced from the review. The run-off owner should be prepared for this to be realistic. This is because the premium quoted will be a one-off amount payable irrespective of the future development of the book. The risk of adverse development is carried in the future by the Reinsurer and the run-off owner is protected up to the reinsurance limit (this is colloquially known as a "no tears cover"). The claims are still administered by the Reinsured, although often via the claims control clause the Reinsurer has the right to be associated with their defence and settlement once the extra reinsurance coverage begins to be utilised.

Obviously, where limited adverse development cover is offered, the risk will be covered only up to a pre-determined level. In some cases, however, the likelihood of a breach of the upper limit is so remote that the cover is almost as good as an unlimited protection. Probably the hardest part of this task would be finding Reinsurers who are financially secure enough to take on long-tail liabilities and are also willing to act as a Reinsurer of last resort. Secondly, depending on the portfolio in run-off, the difficulty of calculating the correct price to be charged for such a cover should not be underestimated.

Advantages

- it is a simple solution;
- it can be implemented quickly;
- it uses the familiar mechanism of a contract of reinsurance;
- depending on the terms, it can offer financial finality at a very competitive price when compared with the cost of finalising the run-off by means of a solvent scheme of arrangement. This is currently reinforced by the cheapness of reinsurance in a soft market;
- from a UK regulatory perspective, the requirements that must be complied with are certainly no more onerous than those required under the solvent scheme mechanism;
- stock market perception of added value;
- advantageous capital treatment by accounting and regulatory authorities (i.e. free up capital to employ elsewhere).

Disadvantages

- the cap on exposure does not alleviate the administrative burden of the run-off;
- limited number of Reinsurers prepared to offer protection on a stop loss basis;
- more reinsurance does not guard against the possibility of a deterioration in the market as a whole;
- there remains the problem of the long-term security of the reinsurers;
- might only be commercially viable once the uncertainty inherent

in the book of business has been reduced (perhaps by a programme of commutations);

- unlimited guarantees and stop loss contracts may be counter-productive in certain circumstances because they make the recipient, for financial evaluation purposes (but not legally), part of the provider, thus hindering commutation talks.

3.5.1.4 Loss portfolio transfer

A loss portfolio transfer is essentially the transfer of liabilities usually between successive years of account in consideration for a premium that is calculated to equate to those liabilities. It is essentially a reinsurance to close the prior treaty year with the new treaty year assuming responsibility for the payment of losses as and when they arise in respect of those prior year liabilities.

We are not concerned here about portfolio transfers found in individual proportional treaties[xviii] where portfolio transfers bring an underwriting year to a close in order to avoid the uneconomic processing of minor amounts. However, the effect is similar – liabilities under a portfolio of risks are transferred from one Reinsurer to another.

Portfolio reinsurance involves the retrocession of the entire portfolio of business to another Reinsurer. The premium charged must be sufficient to pay for all eventual liabilities.

Advantages

- in some cases the premium charged may leave some margin for profit for the shareholders.

Disadvantages

- lack of Reinsurers prepared to offer such protection;

(xviii) Under such treaties unearned premiums or outstanding claims are transferred from one underwriting year to another, with outgoing Reinsurers being debited and incoming Reinsurers credited with a percentage (or other agreed formula) of outstanding claims and unearned premium. Such contracts have regular accounts reflecting the payment of premium and claims. Without Portfolio transfers treaty accounts would continue until all outstanding claims had been settled, which could take many years. This is often a provision in the terms and conditions of a new underwriting year being written, i.e., at some stage to accept the run-off of the book of business written in earlier years.

- it is difficult to accurately estimate IBNR losses so again there will be difficulties in calculating the appropriate premium;
- the company still remains liable for its claims if the ultimate Reinsurer fails to pay out for whatever reason.

3.5.1.5 Alternative risk transfer products

Background

Conventional reinsurance is by no means the only way of managing insurance risk. Risk managers have long been acquainted with financial reinsurance products. They now have available a range of new products which have generically become known as Alternative Risk Transfer (ART).

It is unfortunate that the expression ART has gained common currency since it does not accurately reflect the nature of the products employed. Many of the products involve 'risk financing' in combination with 'risk transfer' and share more of the characteristics of a banking or corporate finance transaction.

The real development of alternative risk transfer with its modern connotation, began in the 1980s with the development of what was originally termed financial reinsurance and became better known as finite risk reinsurance.

What is Finite Risk Reinsurance?

Due to the diversity of the products available, it is difficult to find a generally accepted definition. It is, however, an undisputed fact that finite risk reinsurance represents a combination of risk transfer and risk financing which emphasises the time-value of money. The essential characteristics of Finite Risk solutions, i.e. particularly:

- the assumption of limited (finite) risk by the Reinsurer;
- the multi-year period of contracts;
- the sharing of the results with the client and
- the explicit inclusion of future investment income in the stipulated price.

Offer additional possibilities that are encountering growing interest among insurance companies as well as large corporate clients.

Finite Risk Reinsurance is:

- balancing out of risks;
- over time ;
- in a single relationship between Insurer and Reinsurer;
- by stabilising profits;
- with a tailor-made reinsurance protection;
- and investment income considered in pricing elements.

Benefits of Finite Risk Reinsurance

- protection of the balance sheet and income statement;
- smoothing effect: Severe losses are spread over time;
- predictability of earnings, surplus and loss ratios are improved;
- critical balance sheet ratios can be managed easier;
- capital substitute: The more stable the results are, the less capital is required.

The biggest run-off transactions to date have involved either asbestos and environmental liabilities or workers' compensation[xix].

Definition of ART

ART continues to mean different things to different people. This is partly because products per se do not exist as off-the-shelf products. Instead, certain core building blocks are used to structure solutions. These can be categorised as multiyear (i.e. 2 years or longer), multiline (i.e. integrating several lines of business, thus enhancing diversification), integrated, blended, and double trigger structures. We are concerned here only with those ART solutions which apply to run-off. There are very few. They only involve multiyear structures and combine both risk transfer and risk financing. The risk transfer is limited (finite) to an aggregate or overall limit of liability, often defined by utilising conventional excess of loss methodology. The risk financing recognizes the time value of money so that the Insured are partly funding their own loss experience. (The projected investment income from the premiums is explicitly brought into the calculation of

(xix) Swiss Re *Integrating Corporate Risk Management* October 1999.

the premium). In many ways ART solutions are very similar to their conventional reinsurance counterparts. The fundamental difference is that the ART solution tends to address a host of financial considerations in combination with those relating to pure risk transfer.

In a finite reinsurance, the client has a programme tailored to his or her own claims experience. Finite risk arrangements require the Reinsurer to have a good security rating, because of their multi-year nature. Companies offering finite policies need a variety of skilled personnel: Underwriters; Actuarial staff; Investment staff; Accountants; Claims specialists, and Legal staff. This assists the financial modelling process, which is necessary to evaluate all aspects of the transactions.

To ensure that premiums are regarded as an expense of the business, to be set against or deducted from other tax liabilities, the Inland Revenue requires that there is a genuine risk transfer and not just a spreading of loss over a period of years.

In essence, finite risk contracts are used to protect against potential adverse development on discontinued business.

In the future traditional reinsurance solutions might be partially substituted by these new alternative methods as we witness a convergence of the banking and insurance markets. However, to date, risk financing solutions remain at the fringes of the reinsurance market.

Aon Risk Services UK conducts a biennial Risk Financing Survey, which in 1999 showed that use of finite risk programmes has increased since 1997. Three years ago about 9% of companies responding to the poll said they already use finite risk programmes; the percentage increased to 14% in 1999.

Advantages

- may maximise the value of the business for policyholders and owners. ART attempts to seek the value today rather than waiting for it to appear tomorrow;
- reduces the uncertainty of cash-flows;
- overcomes any investment portfolio constraints related to asset/liability matching;
- provides an income for the company not just for those policyholders with claims today but also for those policyholders with claims in the future;

- achieves certainty.

Disadvantages

- pemiums can be relatively high reflecting the high risk of the contracts;
- these arrangements are more complicated than traditional reinsurance;
- in constructing an ART solution for run-off, considerable work is required by the company with the auditors and tax and legal advisors;

It should be noted that reinsurance run-off solutions could be grouped into two categories:

- pure reinsurance agreements where the liabilities remain with the original party. The object being to strengthen the company's ability to cope with the financial effects of the liabilities e.g.,adverse development covers;
- reinsurance agreements which support the transfer of the run-off liabilities to external partners (any company which retains risk must expect to pay any losses, plus risk handling, plus the opportunity cost of the capital involved, that is the returns available by investing these funds elsewhere.).

3.5.2 Non-insurance solutions

As companies go into run-off, the end result from the shareholder's point of view is that a large amount of capital has been left, trapped, in these companies. Worse still, companies in run-off are frequently a drag on the earnings of their parent organisations.

The owners of such companies look to run-off providers to reduce liabilities and to achieve capital repatriation through either acquisition, financial restructuring or sale to third parties.

Indeed the establishment of Equitas can be seen in these terms. It is indeed a strategy by which Lloyd's Names could close their involvement on syndicates with open underwriting years, free their capital and exit from their underwriting commitments. However, despite the capital release features, it is obviously an insurance-based one, albeit a unique one.

3.5.2.1 Sell the company in run-off or the discontinued book of business

Outside the run-off industry, there has been a spate of mergers and acquisitions in recent years. In 1998 32 mergers or acquisitions took place where the value of transactions exceeded US$500 million and had a total value placed on them of US$87 billion. 133 insurer mergers were announced during the first quarter of 1999 including American International Group's acquisition of Sunamerica Inc. for US$16.87 billion and the Aegon acquisition of Transamerica for US$9.7 billion. The recent merger and acquisition activity has been attributed to major Bermudian Insurers increasing their global presence and major European Insurers which have sought to expand.

Within the run-off industry the motivation of the seller and the buyer will often be different to that in the live market. However, it is difficult to generalise since there can be a whole myriad of motivating factors. The motivation of the seller may be to free himself of uncertain liabilities – he may be looking to rid himself of an encumbrance. Alternatively, he may have concluded that the company was not achieving the return on equity required, and may be looking for a way out of the insurance/reinsurance industry. It should be noted that any company considering the possibility of going into run-off would fare better seeking a buyer before the decision to cease underwriting was actually made. This is because, the company will be able to sell itself as an ongoing insurance/reinsurance organisation which has fought hard for licenses to operate as an Insurer[xx].

The buyer will often be seeking to build a portfolio of difficult books of business (e.g. those with long-term casualty exposures) which he can weld together and hopefully extract hidden value from. (One good example of a well-known buyer of companies in run-off is Berkshire Hathaway). The buyer is incredibly price sensitive, since this will largely determine whether or not it can squeeze its margin out of this company, together with its plan to run the company on a more efficient basis.

In other ways the sale of a company in run-off will be very similar to the sale of any significant company. It will involve the following stages:

- pre-contract – The buyer carries out due diligence (i.e. the process

(xx) The authorisation process can be complex and time consuming, taking between 6 to 9 months. This issue is discussed in greater depth later in this book.

of discovering as much as possible about the business/company as he can). The seller will be required to give the buyer commercially sensitive information relating to the business/company. The seller must ensure that the buyer has signed a confidentiality agreement before any information is given. Heads of agreement may be signed between the buyer and seller which record the main terms agreed between the parties;[xxi]

- signing contracts – Once the acquisition agreement has been agreed both parties will sign it;[xxii]
- completion – buyer will pay the agreed purchase price to the seller (unless there are staged/deferred payments);
- post-completion – the buyer must check that any all necessary legal compliances are carried out such as the writing up of the company's statutory books to reflect the new ownership.

Because of the complex legal issues, lawyers will need to be heavily involved in the process.

A successful sale of a company in run-off requires:

- a willing buyer and seller ;
- an acceptable price – sale of the company is based on its present net value;
- regulatory acceptance i.e. by the Financial Services Authority. The FSA is sensitive to changes of ownership and will examine the buyer's business plan and motivations, and will not agree to the take-over unless the policyholders are no worse off under the new ownership.

Problems

The realities of the sale process can be fraught with problems:

- difficulty regarding the **valuation** of any company in run-off

(xxi) The heads should be expressed to be subject to contract and should contain a provision which clearly states that they are not intended to be legally binding (if this is the intention of the parties). Bearing in mind that the buyer will spend time and money on the due diligence process he is likely to want to enter into a lock-out agreement with the seller whereby the seller agrees not to negotiate with any third parties for a certain period of time.

(xxii) The buyer usually drafts the first draft of the acquisition agreement and it will therefore usually be in his favour.

(since judgements are needed on future claims development, levels of current and future bad debts, outcome of litigation and run-off costs). The biggest problem is assessing the ultimate cost associated with environment and pollution losses, and who will ultimately be asked to pay for these losses. One solution is to involve a Reinsurer offering run-off protection at an early stage in the negotiations who is willing to assume the uncertainty for a given premium;

- it is difficult for the buyer and seller to reach an agreement in which they each consider themselves to be the winner;
- the conflicting objectives of the buyer and the seller;
- agreeing on the price, since the buyer and the seller are viewing the transaction from different perspectives. Buying a company for £1 can be an expensive proposition when the company has huge, and moreover, uncertain liabilities.

The buyer will concentrate on four factors:

- time value of money computations based over a pre-determined period (e.g. a 10-year period). At the end of this term he will hopefully be in a position to withdraw capital from the company;
- discounted valuations of future reinsurance recoveries allowing for future Reinsurer insolvencies and non-payers;
- loading the reserves to allow for IBNR erosion and adverse loss development;
- buyer's profit element for the risk factor and the opportunity cost of capital that is the returns available by investing these funds elsewhere.

The price will be a combination of two main factors:

- The amount of cash the purchaser has and the source of that cash (venture capitalists require higher rates of return).
- Because of the risk premium that the buyer has to add to the equation, it is often the case that the buyer will require an additional capital injection from the parent (or shareholders) before he is willing to buy a company. This often takes the form of a limited guarantee. At this point, negotiations often break down.

Advantages

- the sale of a company offers a complete transfer of all liabilities with no further repercussions;
- it includes the transfer of both the liabilities and the operations of the run-off.

Disadvantages

- insurers with long-tail businesses will find it difficult to find willing purchasers;
- a sale often realises little value;
- if group reinsurance or guarantees are given as part of the sale then financial exposure continues for the seller;
- a sale involves giving up control of the company. Given that the buyer (or his appointed agent) will take over and administer the contracts entered into in the name of the seller, this leaves the seller's reputation at the mercy of a third party's actions;
- adverse publicity is generated where insolvency follows quickly on the heels of a sale.

3.5.2.2 Increase capital

The constraint for a company in run-off is the amount of capital left when adequately reserved. This is the pot of money that has to pay for any increase in the value of inwards claims reported and meet the future administration costs of running-off the business.

The owners of a company in run-off that faces insolvency problems may wish to provide additional financial support by way of refinancing. Alternatively, the shareholders may be prepared to provide additional capital to allow the company to meet its obligations even though, generally speaking, they are under no legal obligation to do so.

Advantages

- the consequences of insolvency will be avoided. This allows control of the company to remain with the Directors and avoids any adverse publicity (so long as there is an ultimate cost benefit in the ultimate determination of the portfolio).

Disadvantages

- refinancing is usually unattractive to investors because new capital would be vulnerable to deterioration on old business and so such Insurers would be at a competitive disadvantage when compared to new Insurers that did not carry the baggage of old risks;
- a refinancing may hinder a run-off's commutations capability (companies which are financially healthy are less attractive commutation targets in general terms and even when approached may be offered less appealing commutation terms than those otherwise obtainable. The ability of the Reinsurer to meet future losses is one of the main factors in determining the price of the commutation);
- only provides a short-term solution if financial losses continue;
- financial support should be linked with a mechanism that creates certainty (such as unlimited adverse loss development cover) and thereby ensures refinancing is never required again.

3.5.2.3 UK – Solvent or Insolvent schemes of arrangement

A UK company can continue to manage itself in a run-off situation as long as there are sufficient net assets to match the solvency requirement. If the net assets are insufficient to meet liabilities at any date, then the company may be put into liquidation or managed under a Scheme of Arrangement.

Definition of Scheme of Arrangement

> **"A compromise or arrangement between a company and its creditors provided for under section 425 of the Companies Act 1985."**

A Scheme of Arrangement is a method by which creditors, in return for giving up certain rights, hope to benefit, perhaps in the short term, perhaps in the longer, by getting more out of the company which is in financial trouble, and more quickly, than would be the case with a full course of insolvent liquidation.

The Scheme of Arrangement process is often used in corporate reorganisations outside the insurance industry. A Scheme provides, in effect, a written constitution setting out in detail the basis upon which the run-off of the company's affairs will be handled. Schemes vary from company to company since each is tailored to meet the precise needs of the company. All schemes share certain common characteristics, including mechanisms for controlling and managing the affairs of the company. A scheme will be managed by a licensed insolvency practitioner who will be appointed scheme administrator. He will be accountable to a committee of creditors and to the creditors.

The term 'run-off' stops being applied to a company upon the company being put into a **Scheme of Arrangement**[xxiii] (whether a solvent scheme or otherwise). The liabilities are no longer run-off until expiry. Rather, under a Scheme of Arrangement the creditors agree to receive a reduced percentage payout of their losses and the liabilities are consequently finalised. It is not an Insolvency Act procedure. The most significant feature of Section 425 is that it provides a mechanism whereby all creditors of the company will be bound even though only 75% in value **and** a simple majority in number of creditors who vote on the scheme approve it, provided that it is subsequently sanctioned by the court.

Under insolvency the liabilities are administered under statute by an insolvency practitioner who calculates the percentage payout of the losses based upon the deficiency of the total assets in relation to the total liabilities. The main difference between these two eventualities is that creditors have some form of control (via their voting rights) under a Scheme of Arrangement, but it is the liquidator who has the control under liquidation. Furthermore a Scheme of Arrangement is a more flexible tool than the dogmatic approach encapsulated within the administration of liquidation (where procedures are set in stone).

It is common practice, as an alternative to liquidation, for the directors or the provisional liquidator of a reinsurance company to propose a Scheme of Arrangement. The number of schemes proposed for insurance companies has increased dramatically as liquidation is

---

(xxiii) There are broadly two types of insolvent Scheme of Arrangement utilised in the London market: run-off schemes and cut-off schemes. Run-off Schemes of Arrangement for insolvent companies mirror the position of a solvent company in run-off, paying claims as and when they fall due. (However, claims are paid at a reduced rate or payment percentage to reflect the shortfall in the assets of the company over its liabilities). KWELM, English & American, Orion, Halvanon, St. Helens, Fremont, Pinetop, ICS Re, RMCA Re are examples. Cut-off schemes are no more than mass commutations. However, they do bring finality to a run-off early. Examples are Scan Re (solvent) and Crombie (insolvent). It should be noted that cut-off schemes are limited in application to those situations where there are predominantly short tail liabilities and limited reinsurance protections. A Scheme does not bind the Reinsurers.

now often considered an inappropriate and expensive way of dealing with an insolvent insurer.

The scheme basically requires establishing a list of creditors and debtors. This is not an easy or quick task, especially where business has been written through a number of different Brokers at home and abroad. This task is also made more difficult as most reinsurance companies maintain their accounts at Broker level rather than at cedant level.

Following adoption of the scheme, policyholders claims are paid at a reduced rate or payment percentage to reflect the shortfall in the assets of the company over its liabilities (e.g. 25% of their claims amount due rather than 100%), and this is known as a dividend rather than a claim payment. However, the company continues to receive its own reinsurance recoveries in full from its own Reinsurers (recent case law has confirmed this right to full recovery).

The most famous example of a scheme of arrangement is the KWELM companies (comprising Kingscroft Insurance, Walbrook Insurance, El Paso Insurance, Lime Street Insurance, and Mutual Reinsurance) which are subsidiaries of the failed London United Investments plc. Ian Bond and Chris Hughes, of Coopers & Lybrand[xxiv], were appointed administrators of the scheme of arrangement for the insolvent KWELM insurance companies in 1993. The KWELM companies ceded business to over 700 Reinsurers with their books of business, including US casualty, product liability and professional indemnity risks. At December 31 1995, possible overall liabilities of the KWELM companies were estimated at around $9.7bn, including a ‘special margin’ of $4.4bn for certain long-tail business.

Advantages

- as compared with a liquidation:

  (a) there are no detailed rules for the content of schemes, enabling an insolvent Insurer to devise the most appropriate method for achieving an orderly settlement of its affairs; It permits greater flexibility to deal with a business where it is both unlikely that all creditors are identifiable or that all claims are quantifiable at the date of winding up. This difficulty is particularly acute, of course, for companies writing long-tail business where claims may not materialise for a number of years;

(xxiv) Now PricewaterhouseCoopers.

(b) it permits greater flexibility when considering what action could be taken to protect the interests of creditors (for example, a scheme may provide for payments to be made in the currency of claims, thus minimising creditor's exposure to fluctuations in exchange rates);

(c) a scheme may allow for the earlier payment of distributions to creditors;

(d) it is possible to devise a method of resolving disputed claims which may produce substantial cost savings (disputed claims under liquidations tend to be litigated with the liquidator);

(e) investment and handling of a company's cash assets will not be subject to the fees and levies payable in accordance with statutory requirements applicable in a liquidation;

(f) an investment policy may be adopted which is suitable to the security, liquidity, and yield requirements of a particular company;

(g) terminates the run-off – The use of insolvent liquidation and Schemes of Arrangement has provided the biggest exit route for companies exiting run-off;

(h) all cedants are bound despite the fact that less than 100% vote in favour of the scheme. The ability to bind all creditors is a very important feature in relation to insurance/reinsurance companies where even the identity of creditors in some cases, and certainly the actual value of most creditors' claims, may be unknown when the votes are taken.

Disadvantages

- there are some disadvantages of a scheme as compared with a liquidation, the most important of which are the loss of the extensive investigative powers of a liquidator and certain unique remedies in law which a liquidator has against directors;[xxv]
- it is a complex arrangement because of the level of due diligence required coupled with the detailed drafting which goes into the scheme document;
- it may encompass a significant amount of delay whilst the scheme

(xxv) For example where there has been wrongful or fraudulent trading or where there have been voidable preferences or transactions at an undervalue.

is being drafted and agreed by the policyholders and the courts. It often takes from 12 to 36 months;

- it is expensive since it involves substantial legal work and approval from the courts;
- it may hamper the ability to recover from Reinsurers if the scheme is badly drafted;
- it cannot of course bind the company's Reinsurers to its terms.

Solvent Schemes of Arrangements.

Such schemes are intended to prevent companies that have been run-off for many years being forced into provisional liquidation at the tail end of the run-off, but rather bring up front a scheme which will be endorsed by the court at a time when the directors are satisfied that the company is **capable of meeting its known liabilities** (but cannot predict the future uncertainties inherent in dealing with long-tail business).

The scheme manager seeks to place a scheme before the courts whereby all claims are **paid in full** with a full and final settlement; the payment will incorporate paid claims, agreed outstandings and IBNR.

Advantages

- it brings finalisation and therefore avoids adverse claims deterioration;
- cuts off run-off administration costs;
- provides the opportunity to return shareholder equity earlier than would otherwise have been the case had the company remained in run-off;
- senior management time is freed from focusing upon run-off issues;
- in essence, capital and reserves are paid to policyholders rather than being absorbed by attritional run-off expense and devaluing reinsurance assets;
- all interested parties get their money within, say, a three year time period of the scheme being agreed, earlier if the scheme is not too complex;

- avoids the payment of Insolvency Services Agency fees, which are regarded by some as a tax on creditors in a liquidation. (In essence the ISA charges statutory fees both on the value of assets realised by a liquidator and on investments made by him, which he is required to make through the Insolvency Service);
- when the portfolio remaining after major commutations is relatively small the effect of a solvent scheme will be to commute with the remaining Reinsurers at a fair price. Small commutations may drag on for years and cost a lot of money in terms of management time and administration costs;
- facilitates the valuation of all liabilities on a fair and consistent basis, enabling policyholders to be paid in full and obtain finality.

Disadvantages

- insurance companies considering this route must be confident that they are solvent: there could be nothing worse than to commission a full actuarial valuation, as part of the scheme process, only to find that the company is insolvent;
- there is a relatively high cost to establish and administer such schemes;
- this solution is not suitable for all portfolios.

3.5.2.4 Segregation of the liabilities

Some companies have decided to segregate the liabilities into a separate division. This is a strategic decision which can only be used in the context of a group of companies which retain an interest in the live market.

They hope that by controlling the liability separately within the corporation they could focus better on the problem and develop expertise to handle the risks. More specifically they hope:

- to improve financial results for the current ongoing business by *quantifying* the old liabilities with finality and *segregating* them for run-off; To gain competitive advantage – by quantifying the old liabilities that are resulting in earnings "drag", a company can allocate capital to address the pre-existing liabilities, thereby freeing the remaining surplus for allocation to the ongoing operation. In addition to surplus allocation, more specialised management and personnel allocations can be made. With these changes, it is likely that more favourable ratings will be assigned to the on-going company that helps to attract new capital and improve market position.

By separating the liabilities they believe that it would have no negative impact on new business activity.

This approach offers an operational solution, but not a financial solution or the finalization of liabilities.

A further development on this tactic is to *ring-fence* the liabilities by putting them into a separate company. This attempts to put more space between the current organisation and the old liabilities, so that the ongoing company can operate with a clean bill of health.

This technique offers an effective solution in that the new company is a separate legal entity. However, it is unlikely that such a solution would gain **regulatory** approval in the UK due to the fact that policyholders would be much worse off under the new arrangement.

3.5.2.5 Statutory transfer of the book of business under Schedule 2C Insurance Companies Act

Here we are concerned with the assumption by another Reinsurer of old years' liabilities by way of a statutory transfer of the portfolio of business under Schedule 2C of the Insurance Companies Act 1982 (the 'Act')

The Act provides that an insurance or reinsurance company may with the requisite consent effect a statutory transfer of insurance or reinsurance business. The effect is to transfer the ultimate liability for the business written from the transferor to the transferee. Thus the parties effectively sever the link at law between the legal entity initially writing the business and the actual business written.

The Act contains various safeguards principally aimed at protecting policyholders, in particular the transfer of general business requires the approval of the Treasury and the transfer of long-term business the approval of the High Court.

Unfortunately, there are legal and practical problems to implementing such proposals. The major issue concerns the transferability of the reinsurance protection. The reinsurance protection does not transfer automatically. It can therefore only protect the transferred business if it can be assigned at the same time.

Alternatively, the consent of the all the Reinsurers involved in the reinsurance programme for the company must be sought. Secondly, such transfers depend on the willingness of the Financial Services Authority to approve the transfer. The effect of a statutory transfer would be to deprive policyholders of their rights to claim against the original Underwriters of the policy. The **regulator** will only approve it where the policyholders are no worse off after the transfer.

Statutory transfer is commonly used for inter-group and intra-group transfers of insurance or reinsurance business.

For the Reinsurer assuming such portfolios, the assumption of liabilities from more than one source on the same business gives the opportunity for economies of scale to be achieved.

Advantages

- can be used for just part of a book of business (i.e. contracts of a certain nature);
- it transfers both the exposure and administrative expense in one procedure;
- can be implemented quickly, if there are not too many Reinsurer consents to be obtained.

Disadvantages

- the major issue concerns the transferability of the reinsurance protection. The reinsurance protection does not transfer automatically;
- might only be commercially viable once the uncertainty inherent in the book of business has been reduced (perhaps by a programme of commutations);
- less likelihood of future unravelling of arrangements or disputes.

3.5.2.6 A combination of solutions – the customised approach

Depending upon the make up of the portfolio; the owner's attitude to risk; the owner 's core competencies; the owner's financial health; the relative cost of the different solutions; the general state of the live market and the run-off market, it may be appropriate to choose more than one solution to deal with retrospective liabilities.

For example:

1. A combination of whole account stop loss and a statutory transfer.
2. A two-stage strategy:
   - pro-active run-off until the run-off has reached a stage where the major contracts have been commuted and the amount of uncertainty regarding ultimate liabilities has been brought within acceptable parameters;
   - followed by a finalization of liabilities using a Solvent Scheme of Arrangement or finite reinsurance.
3. Buying a large amount of whole account stop loss during the first year of run-off, and then pursuing a passive run-off approach thereafter.

3.6 Implement – Stage 4

Naturally the plan adopted will vary from company to company since each is tailored to meet the precise needs of the company. However, once the plan has been designed it needs to be expertly implemented.

Procedures and protocols will need to be put into place to enable the implementation process to occur smoothly and without any unforeseen problems. Again, the emphasis is upon anticipating problems rather than waiting for them to happen.

Whatever plan is adopted it will be important for the company to

- involve Reinsurers in implementing the plan as the reinsurance programme will be one of the companies largest assets. It will be important to;
  - (a) be aware of their largest Reinsurers – are they solvent; are they dispute-orientated; are they in run-off ?
  - (b) monitor reinsurance security;
  - (c) monitor bad-debt write downs;
- involve the **regulator** in implementing the plan;
- be aware of their largest policyholders – are they dispute-orientated?

3.7 Review – Stage 5

Progress should be monitored against the plan and the budget with targets and a timetable in place. The strategy should be reviewed and revised on an annual basis dependent upon the progress made in the interim to ensure that the strategy is relevant to the current state of the external business environment. This review process is often overlooked

There is no substitute for periodic reviews. At least part of this could come through the internal audit function, particularly in larger companies. Some companies have a business planning department which, in addition to managing the business planning process, carries out financial evaluation and performance analysis.

However, where specialised reinsurance knowledge is required, outsourcing to specialists could be necessary, unless personnel with the relevant skills can be seconded from other parts of the organisation.

Elements of the review:

The review should be tailored to its specific objectives but should include the following:

- adequacy and soundness of reinsurance asset quality, loss reserving adequacy, adequacy of capital;
- systems and processes;
- claims procedures and controls;
- outwards reinsurance mechanisms;
- accounting systems and financial reporting;
- the quality and estimated market value of assets should be reviewed to determine the effects of their sudden, unexpected and enforced sale.

Obviously such annual reviews will be considered in conjunction with:

- monthly management accounts;
- annual financial audits;
- ad-hoc internal reviews carried out by the internal audit function;
- monthly material claim listings.

Examples of revised strategy

Two good examples of a revised strategy are:

- the revolutionary use of solvent Schemes of Arrangement in recent times. – HIR[xxvi] UK was the first to use this procedure in 1998;
- Equitas use of 'materiality projects' which aim to attack low value, high cost processes;
  - they introduced reinsurance claim collecting note thresholds of $25,000 which immediately removed 56% of their outward reinsurance claims processing whilst delaying recovery of only 7% of their receivables;
  - they have placed a large number of syndicates into what they term "cold storage" – for these syndicates where the reinsurance asset is small; processing is carried out just once per year.

(xxvi) HIR solvent scheme paid 110% of reserves and agreed IBNR to ensure success with creditors. Shareholders agreed the cost because of the margin of assets over liabilities.

CHAPTER 4: MANAGEMENT AND ORGANISATION

The performance of a company is a factor of its structure and the behaviour of the workforce.

4.1 General Considerations

Each company needs its own organisational structure designed for their unique business objectives and portfolio.

In a run-off situation, although no active underwriting takes place, there exist a whole multitude of tasks still to be performed. The technical and financial processing continue to be carried out, In addition, there are various internal and external reporting requirements. These include:

- Financial Services Authority – Insurers are required to submit audited annual returns to the FSA within six months after the period to which they relate. The annual return demonstrates the solvency of the Insurer. Financial and statistical analyses are included of the solvency position, assets and liabilities, profit and loss account and the underwriting revenue account by class of business;
- annual reports and accounts – Companies incorporated in the UK must prepare financial accounts to be drawn up for a period of one year unless there is a change in the year end and the external auditors are required to consider and report on the adequacy of the claims reserves.[i] Copies of statutory accounts are filed at Companies House within seven months of the accounting reference date, which is extended to ten months in the case of a private company, and are available to the public. The statutory accounts must also be sent free of charge to each shareholder and the Regulator;
- management information requirements – Management will require information (such as the level of claims reserves) for the following reasons:

  (a) to assess the overall financial performance of the company and to measure this against the performance expected;

(i) The annual report and accounts will provide information to many other users/ amongst whom are: competitors – to assess the company's profitability and to provide information for competitive benchmarking; insurance and reinsurance brokers – to assess the security of the company; companies looking to grow by merger or acquisition – to assess the value and financial viability of the company.

(b) to assess run-off expenses and to measure these against those anticipated;

(c) to assess a commutation price.[ii]

In addition to efficient organisation, the following factors are important in trying to manage the portfolio effectively:

1. Employees and Directors must be of the highest quality possible.
2. Teams have to be supported by adequate information and systems resources.
3. Teams require professional management support. It is sometimes said that good management technique is boring in that it involves anticipating; predicting; and preventing problems.

A mixture of claims; legal; accounting; actuarial; organisational; and technical skills are required to manage a run-off. In addition, public relations and negotiating skills are necessary. The CEO must be able to present his run-off organisation in the best possible light and employ staff who are able to negotiate deals to cut off the liability at an acceptable price and within a predetermined timescale.

4.2 Departmental Organisation

The organisation and management of a company in run-off will ultimately depend on:

1. The size of the portfolio being run-off.
2. The type of portfolio being run-off.
3. The stage of the run-off, i.e. beginning – middle – end.
4. The amount of resources available, both financial and human. At the one extreme is the large run-off organisation with 1000 employees and at the other is the one-man operation (in the literal sense).

For bigger run-off concerns the structure is more complex and the tasks that each individual has more delineated and defined.

In the smaller companies one person will necessarily fulfil two or more roles and should therefore be multi-talented. Such people are accountants or lawyers in many cases.

(ii) This is an agreement between a Reinsured and Reinsurer whereby the Reinsurer agrees to pay the Reinsured a sum of money to bring the reinsurance contract to an end

We have seen that an organisation in run-off has the following key success factors:

- increase income;
- decrease expense;
- increase assets;
- decrease liabilities;
- return capital to shareholders;
- control cash-flow;
- stay abreast of company statutory reporting requirements.

The table below shows the department responsible for delivering each of the success factors:

Success Factor	*Department*
Increase income	*Investment*
Decrease expense	*Finance*
Increase assets	*Commutation and Outwards Claims*
Decrease liabilities	*Commutations and Inwards Claims*
Return capital to shareholders	*All departments; especially Planning and Finance*
Control cash-flow	*Finance*
Stay abreast of company statutory reporting requirements	*Finance and Legal*

Table 10 – The success factors of an organisation in run-off and the department responsible for delivering them.

Every company of whatever size will require some sort of organisational structure, whether this is adhered to in practice or not. For example, even a group of ten people in a partnership will have an organisational structure in place in order to enable them to meet their stated business objectives in an efficient manner. Such a structure will define such things as:

- the division of work;
- the chain of command;
- the type of tasks performed;

- the internal groupings which undertake similar work; and the management hierarchy.

There are two main ways to structure a company's departments:

- by function (e.g. claims, legal; finance); and
- by division (e.g. geographical area, type of policyholder etc.).

Structure based on function is the traditional form of insurance company organisation and it is this structure which is best suited to companies in run-off. This is because it has the advantage that employees can specialise in the type of work they carry out since all those employed in the same or related activity form one department. The disadvantages are perhaps the inflexibility of the structure: for example, the claims personnel tend to see their role as purely claims handling and may not recognise their commutation support roles.

In a run-off situation, there is an increased need for:

- good communication and co-operation between the various departments, and this is especially so between the inwards and outwards claims department and the commutations department. This is because there are often both inwards and outwards relationships with particular Reinsurers. Ahard stance of the claims department on inwards claims will often provoke an aggressive stance by the Reinsurer on a company's outward claims;
- good co-ordination of the different functions. Two examples are given:
  - (a) in most cases there is little point in pursuing legal proceedings against a Reinsurer where commutation discussions are taking place. In this situation, co-ordination between the legal department and the commutations department is necessary;
  - (b) because a company in run off will have limited capital and funds available to settle claims, it is important that claim settlement procedures are implemented to ensure that settlements are reviewed and authorised prior to distribution of funds. Otherwise a run-off company may experience cash flow problems. The basic requirements may be that the claims being settled are not under query by the run-off company (or subject to litigation or arbitration); there are no current commutation negotiations with the Reinsured; and that the Reinsured is solvent. In order to implement such procedures requires co-ordination between the Claims Department, the Commutations Department and the Accounting Department.

Use of outsourcing

In both the large and small organisations certain functions will be outsourced. Indeed, in certain instances the whole of the run-off function will be outsourced. Depending on the expertise available in-house, the following maybe outsourced:[iii]

- the whole of the run-off function – in such a case, an independent agent or third party run-off manager is appointed to take responsibility for the administration of the business while the run-off owner retains liability for settlement of claims. The principal advantage may be that it is cheaper than setting-up an in-house facility. The staff required could be more profitably used elsewhere. However, the contract which transfers administrative control must clearly define the responsibilities of the run-off manager and the nature and extent of the authority which is being delegated so that the run-off owner retains effective control;
- claims services;
- legal services;
- investment services;
- actuarial services;
- IT services (for example, Equitas has outsourced its IT services to ITNET – this company now manages Equitas' applications, development services and IT operations);
- inspections of records and technical reinsurance advice;
- recovery of reinsurance collections;
- long-term business planing (i.e. use of management consultants).

Outsourcing is a phenomenon of the 1990's, which have seen organisations concentrating on their core activities and using the skilled services of external companies as needed. Real core activities are those which make the company unique. The two driving forces behind the use of outsourcing are:

- perceived cost benefits; and
- access to a wider skills base.

(iii) Outsourcing is using a skilled resource outside the company to handle work traditionally performed by in-house staff. In essence, a function (or a component thereof) is delegated to a third party by either farming the work out or bringing the resource into the company.

Run-off companies have turned to outsourcing to help them survive the available skill shortage, the effects of fast-changing technology; and narrow margins. Where the whole of the run-off function is being considered for outsourcing, the company in run-off must give attention to each area of requirement and the costs thereof and monitor these on a formal basis. One fundamental question to be considered is whether the run-off should be staffed by people who worked on the account when it was live, or handled exclusively by a third party administrator seeking to make a profit. Choosing the correct third party administrator is a difficult decision, but choosing the incorrect one can be a costly.

4.3 Possible Departmental Structure

Outlined below is one possible departmental structure with a thumbnail sketch of their responsibilities.

4.3.1 Commutations Department [iv]

- initiating commutation discussions with Reinsurers;
- comparing the company's outward reinsurance contracts with those contract details supplied by the Reinsurer;
- negotiating commutation deals;
- co-ordinating the other departments who support the commutation efforts such as the reserving department, the in-house legal department, and the inwards claims department.

A commutation strategy alone cannot achieve finality, but will play a part in controlling exposure and cost. An important element in devising such a strategy will be the correct identification of commutation targets, and a prioritisation of such targets. Another key aspect is the willingness of the counterparty to commute – if willingness is demonstrated then the commutation is likely to be concluded in a relatively short space of time, the main sticking point being finding the correct price. However, if there is reluctance (or perhaps uncertainty)on the part of the one of the parties involved then a lot resource and time may be wasted.

(iv) A commutation is an agreement between a Reinsured and Reinsurer whereby the Reinsurer agrees to pay the Reinsured a sum of money to bring the reinsurance contract to an end

There are three purposes behind negotiating commutations of inwards contracts. These are as follows:[v]

(a) mitigate losses where results are bad;

(b) cut-off tail where development is long;

(c) reduce expenses by cutting administration costs.

Commutations have the advantage of extinguishing liability (and the weaker a company's capital base the stronger its negotiating position), but may require cash to be paid out earlier, thus reducing reserves and thus investing income. In most cases however, a well-considered commutation strategy will be an integral part of a run-off company's overall strategy since it reduces the uncertainty that the company faces.

One possible pitfall regarding commutations is to offer a better deal (in terms of the discount offered on unpaid claims) to those Reinsurers who dispute outward claims presentations or are otherwise slow payers. Because of the incestuous nature of the reinsurance market (where news spreads quickly), such overtly discriminatory behaviour may have the effect of encouraging more Reinsurers to slow the payment of reinsurance claims. Such problems tend to be encountered in large organisations where the commutation process is carried out by different departments (such as the legal department) in addition to the commutations department. Therefore, a commutation strategy should ensure that a reasonably consistent approach is taken by an organisation.

4.3.2 Inwards Claims Department

Responsibilities:

- validating and recording of inwards claims – their basic function is to review, agree and decline claims presented ;
- coding inwards claims by event, class and type of business in order to aid reinsurance recovery;
- record and produce data in respect of gross claims reported to the company.

Given the importance of controlling claims costs to a run-off, the Inwards Claims Department requires high levels of expertise. Inward claims must be handled efficiently and adequately in order to:

(v) See Simon Wilkinson *Why reinsurers use commutations*, Insurance Day

- restrict claim payments to those which are properly due under the terms and conditions of the particular reinsurance contract at issue (it should be noted that there is no such thing as a standard reinsurance contract) and any relevant legal requirements;
- confine claim payments to those which are correctly presented in terms of such technicalities as arithmetic accuracy; adequate loss detail; and any required supporting evidence;
- maintain accurate and representative statistical records of the losses advised; settled; and reserved;
- annually review claim reserves and Letters of Credit ("LOC's"). LOC's should be updated annually by the Reinsured, but it is worth noting that reductions in reserves and cash will not be sent so quickly to those in run-off and it is for the run-off company to follow this up. Likewise claim reserves will require an active review with a diary system affected to maintain current figures. A large number of the company's assets can be tied up needlessly in these two areas.

One of the primary characteristics of a company in run-off is the absence of pressure to make decisions regarding claim settlements based upon a desire to retain the book of business. In a run-off situation there is a general impression in the market that the assets of the run-off entity are limited and can run out at an undetermined point in time. This usually results in more economic and equitable settlements as compared to an on-going operation. As such, claim decisions are made with a view to the economics of any given settlement taking into account the time value of money, where appropriate.

4.3.3 In-house Legal Department

Responsibilities:

- general legal services including taking legal proceedings against slow-paying reinsurers, and drafting commutation agreements;
- complying with various regulations.

4.3.4 Reserving Department

Responsibilities:

- supporting the commutations department in their work;
- assessing the company's reinsurance liabilities;
- monitoring the company's reserves;

- asset and liability modelling to support investment strategy.

Accurate claims reserving is required for three principal reasons:

- HM Treasury reporting requirements, as outlined above;
- for internal and external reporting purposes;
- for monitoring financial performance.

4.3.5 Internal Audit Department

Responsibilities:

- examining and evaluating business processes and procedures;
- providing analyses and recommendations to ensure that business objectives are achieved.

4.3.6 Finance Department

The Finance Department has a more important role when a company is in run-off due to the emphasis upon cash flow and the control of administration costs. Other than the cash generated from its claims, reinsurance recoveries and investment performance (and to a very limited extent from return premiums and commissions), there is no alternative revenue stream.

For example, it is likely that administration costs will be calculated on a per claim basis so that the company can keep a close eye on its expenses.

Furthermore, there is more focus upon unallocated cash in a run-off situation. A company cannot afford to have a large amount of unallocated cash since the margins are much tighter.

It should be noted that an inefficient back-office could sink the company just as easily as adverse claims detoriation.

4.3.6.1 Accounting

This includes financial reporting and cash management. In run-off, accounting should be moved from a compliance, back-office function, to a front-line position within the organisation. This will focus the management's attention on the importance of cash flow. Functions:

- accounting and reconciliation of reinsurance transactions;
- assessing the financial health of Reinsurers;

- reconciliation of Broker statements with the company's statements;
- maintaining accounting ledgers with Cedants, Brokers, Reinsurers, Banks, non-insurance creditors and debtors.

4.3.6.2 Investment management

Functions:

- managing the company's investment portfolios;
- ensuring that the company has sufficient liquidity to meet its obligations as they fall due (otherwise it is insolvent).

4.3.6.3 Security department

Responsibilities:

- maintain information on the financial strength of Cedants and Reinsurers – the main source of information would be the rating agencies, the media and market knowledge;
- consider whether the reviewed company's current or future ability to settle their debts is questionable

In the current economic climate, the stability of Reinsurers is a key issue and a run-off company must be able to act quickly to protect its position in the event of a threatened insolvency. At the extreme, run-off companies can have up to 3,000 Reinsurers on their reinsurance programmes over a 50-year underwriting period making this a full time activity.

4.3.7 Outwards Claims Department

Duties:

- maintaining details of each retrocession contract;
- maintaining up-to-date and accurate information concerning the reinsurance collections due to the company;
- aggregating inwards claims for the purpose of outwards recovery;
- producing and issuing collection notes for Reinsurers (via Brokers);
- ensuring reinsurance recoveries are maximised;
- collecting reinsurance recoveries and pursuing slow payers.

A company in run-off should focus on improving cash flow and collecting any reinsurance recoveries due to them. Recoveries from retrocession covers will be potentially significant and should be addressed as a matter of priority.

The Outwards Claims Department will need to review the types of covers purchased, the limits of liability, classes of business covered and assess how much protection has already been collected and how much remains compared to the potential losses. There have been several examples of run-off companies being wound up due to exhausted retrocession protection.

Adequate computer systems are obviously a pre-requisite to effective reinsurance recoveries. Computer systems can often be offered by third party run-off providers at a smaller cost, but the hidden costs are that it is not so mobile hence tying the company to that specific provider. Run-off companies are often caught by the dilemma that existing computer systems are outdated and inflexible but new systems are too costly. Critically, most old systems do not have principal to principal accounting.

One area which changes upon entering run-off is the level of support from the Brokers in terms of billing and collection of funds from Reinsurers on a timely basis. This is an important area and warrants frequent visits to the Brokers offices to build and maintain good relations. Consolidation of all recoveries through one or a limited number of Brokers on a fee basis, based upon a prompt collection and settlement service, may prove very beneficial and cost effective. However, it should be noted that the outwards Broker has already received one fee for the contract (being the brokerage paid by the company at placement of the reinsurance contract) and to receive a claim collection fee in addition may be viewed as slightly impertinent. One alternative, where appropriate, is for companies to dispense with the services of the Broker and collect directly from its Reinsurers.

4.3.8 Personnel Department

Functions:

- recruitment of staff; setting salaries and additional perks; and relations between employees;
- providing training and career development;
- reviewing staff annual appraisals.

4.3.9 IT Department

Responsibility:

- providing computer system strategy and support.

The computer system requirements of a company in run-off will be different from those of an ongoing company. The underwriting system geared to supporting underwriting decisions and tracking the profitability of risks will become obsolete, however improvements may be required in the claims, credit control and retrocession systems. In each case the system will have to be geared towards control of claim costs and cash flow. An ability to analyse the likely cash flow during the period of run-off is essential. Operational systems may need radical restructuring, for example to provide a ledger at principal level to support reinsurance collections

Some things though will not change, the system will still have to be able to not only, record the level of information required, but also to report this information to management, speedily and in a usable format.

Computer system considerations

Control of costs will be a vital consideration prior to any changes in the system. Management will have to consider whether any changes warrant the additional costs. In some instances an update in the hardware and/or software system may be unavoidable in order to achieve efficient reporting. In most cases, money spent on an efficient computer system is money well spent since it allows the company in run-off to retain control of its business and most importantly, of its cash-flow.

The following are some of the data issues that a company in run-off will need to review in relation to their existing system or when considering alternatives:

- what level of information is recorded?
- what level of data output is provided?
- how flexible is the system?
- how easily can the data be manipulated?
- how easily can the data be related to other systems?
- is data input into one system or many? (e.g. is there duplication of data entry?)
- what system is there to maintain data and control data input?
- is the system reliable?
- is it better to purchase an off-the-shelf or tailor-made software package?

Data quality

The importance of the accuracy of the data cannot be overstated. Any material errors, for example in codings, will severely affect the accuracy of the analysis performed. Data quality is a particular problem for reinsurance companies in run-off where:

- the volume of data is very large;
- outside contractors are used to process reinsurance transactions;
- the records of more than one reinsurance organisation have been amalgamated; and
- the analysis of the data currently required is beyond that originally contemplated.

Although compensating adjustments may be made, a significant data quality issue may, at the extreme, result in the reinsurance organization's financial report and accounts being qualified by the auditors.

4.4 Setting Objectives for Each Department

As well as setting company-wide objectives, it is important also to set specific departmental objectives. This has similar effects at the departmental level as it does at the company-wide level i.e.

- it establishes clear goals;
- it forms a benchmark against which a department can measure itself;
- it motivates the staff to increase their productivity.

If the departmental objectives are linked directly to remuneration the staff within that department are motivated to perform well and feel that their efforts are recognised. However, where unrealistic objectives are set these can act as a demotivating factor.

In short, such objectives should be:

- S – Specific;
- M – Measurable;
- A – Achievable;
- R – Realistic;
- T – Timebounded.

This system is known as setting SMART objectives.

For example, the following could be an objective for the commutations department:

> *"Subject to commercial considerations, by the end of 2001, the commutations department will have completed (and received funds relating thereto) commutations worth £100,000 (i.e. £100,000 of reinsurance recoveries)"*

The above figure can then be measured every quarter, and reasons for the under (or over) achievement sought. If underachievement is occurring, remedies can be sought and implemented if possible. Such objectives need to be implemented in a common sense way. For example, the above objective, without the qualification regarding commercial considerations, would focus solely upon short-term financial gains.

When carried out in a focused manner, the task of managing a company in run-off can be every bit as challenging and rewarding as running a live company. Indeed, given the fact that there are so many inherent problems (in the portfolio itself; in the unexpected legal and technical problems which tend to arise when retrospective liabilities are closely examined; and in the negative reaction of some members of the reinsurance community such as particular Brokers), the task of controlling a run-off can be a very rewarding experience. The person in charge of a run-off is able to experiment with new ideas as to how best to tackle the problems at hand and can see results quite quickly. The scope for innovation is very wide.

CHAPTER 5: THE ROLE OF THE REGULATOR

5.1 Introduction

Continuing deregulation and harmonisation of Europe is removing barriers to existing markets. An Insurer whose head office is in a European Union ("EU") member state and authorised to write insurance business in their home member state may operate anywhere in the EU under a single licence. Consequently, companies no longer need an authorisation to conduct business in each member state, although there are notification procedures to be followed before an EU Insurer can provide insurance services into the UK. Reinsurers are regulated in the UK so, in order to provide reinsurance only into the UK, a Reinsurer must be authorised to write direct business in its home member state.[i]

It is commonly recognised that the UK has a highly developed and well-regulated insurance/reinsurance industry. In particular, London has an unrivalled wealth of experience and expertise.

5.2 The Need for Regulation of Insurance and Reinsurance Companies[ii]

In the UK, the ultimate objective of the Financial Services Authority ("FSA") in the regulation of insurance and reinsurance companies can be simply stated as being:

> **"The protection of policyholders (or potential policyholders) of insurance/reinsurance companies against the risk that the company may be unable to meet its liabilities"**
>
> *(Insurance Companies Act 1982 s. 37 (2)).*

All of its subsidiary aims are based on this primary objective.

The FSA seeks to control insurance/reinsurance companies in order to protect the following groups:

- policyholders;
- third parties.

We shall look at both of these in turn:

(i) See *Insurance in the UK – a guide to authorisation* Deloitte & Touche 1999.

(ii) For more on this subject, see *The application of Reinsurance*, Chartered Insurance Institute, May 1999. Edited by Peter Wedge.

Policyholders

The **FSA**, on behalf of the UK Government seeks to protect consumers by ensuring that Insurers are able to pay claims when they arise. Unlike other products, the quality of insurance is only determinable when something goes wrong. It is then too late to remedy an imperfect product. Regulation aims to ensure that the product will respond. The procedure used for regulating Insurers and Reinsurers is the:

- establishment of solvency;
- monitoring of solvency.

The regulation process is applied at all stages of an insurance/ reinsurance company's life i.e.

- seeking licenses to write business;
- ongoing monitoring whilst writing business;
- closer monitoring after licenses to write business have been withdrawn.

Naturally, the **FSA** pays closer attention to companies once they are regarded by the **FSA** as being financially impaired or otherwise suspected of not being able to pay their claims in full as they fall due. The regulation of reinsurance companies is very similar to that of insurance. In addition to regulating the insurance/reinsurance companies to ensure they remain solvent there is additional legislation in the UK, which provides a mechanism for compensating policyholders of failed Insurers. The actual legislation is the Policyholders Protection Act 1975. This act established the Policyholders Protection Board (PPB).[iii] Under the terms of this Act 'protected policyholders' – in most circumstances, individuals (i.e. natural persons), or partnerships comprised wholly of individuals with claims under 'United Kingdom policies' are paid 90% of their valid claims and, in cases of compulsory insurance classes 100%.[iv]

(iii) It should be noted that Lloyd's policyholders are in a slightly better position than policyholders with other insurance/reinsurance providers in terms of security since Lloyd's Central Fund provides policyholders with wider coverage against default than that offered by the Policyholders Protection Board.

(iv) Under the terms of a Scheme of Arrangement it is *possible* that the PPB would agree to be bound by the Scheme and (if the Scheme paid less than 90%) would make an additional payment to 'protected policyholders' to bring the total and maximum sum paid up to 90%.

Third Parties

Third parties who suffer loss as a result of the fault of policyholders protected by liability insurance also have an indirect interest in ensuring that the insurer/reinsurer can pay claims, particularly when the date of payment may come many years after the policy was purchased, as happens in long-tail liability insurance business. The third party will have a claim against the policyholder who in turn seeks recovery from his insurance company.

5.3 Types of Regulation

There are four types of direct regulation:

- solvency margin;
- suitability of Directors and Officers;
- ownership of insurance companies;
- company regulation.

1. Solvency margin

There is no minimum requirement for share capital, as Insurers need to demonstrate that they have adequate financial resources. Regulation to ensure the financial security of companies in the UK is based on solvency, which is measured by the excess of admissible assets over liabilities. Insurers are required to maintain a minimum margin of solvency for both long term and general business

If the company's actual margin of solvency is less than the required margin of solvency it will need to submit to the FSA a plan for the restoration of a sound financial position. This is arguably the most important tool in the Regulator's toolbox and especially in the context of discontinued business where 'financial health' is often an issue.

2. Suitability of Directors and Officers

Each director, controller, manager must be a fit and proper person to hold that position and be approved by the Regulator. The FSA will also look at the collective insurance experience of the board and senior management. There is a requirement that Insurers conduct their business in accordance with the criteria of sound and prudent management having due regard to the interests of policyholders. The business of the Insurer must be carried on with integrity, due care and the professional skills appropriate to the nature and scale of its activities. In the context of run-off the criteria of sound and prudent management will be important prior to taking the decision to cease underwriting. The criteria of being a fit and proper person will be significant upon a change of ownership.

3. Ownership of insurance companies

Regulations exist to control changes of ownership. In the UK this is achieved directly by s.61A of the Insurance Companies Act 1982 and indirectly by the Competition Act 1998.

4. Company regulation

Insurance companies, being companies, are regulated in the same way that ordinary companies are regulated. The majority of the applicable regulations are contained in the Companies Act 1985. Companies incorporated in the UK must prepare financial accounts to be drawn up for a period of one year unless there is a change in the year-end. In addition, Insurers are required to submit audited annual returns to the FSA within six moths after the period to which they relate. The annual return demonstrates the solvency of the Insurer. Financial and statistical analyses are included of the solvency position, assets and liabilities, profit and loss account and the underwriting revenue account by class of business.

5.4 Authorisation of Insurers

No company is allowed to carry on insurance business in the UK unless it is authorised to do so in accordance with the requirements set out in The Insurance Companies Act 1982. Authorisation is granted for specific classes of insurance.

The Department of Trade and Industry and the Department of Trade were the ***Regulators*** *before 1997 and 1983 respectively. More recently, the Treasury Insurance Directorate was briefly the Regulator before the empowering of the FSA.*

In order to obtain authorisation, a company must submit a proposal showing how it will carry on business, providing detailed financial forecasts for the first 3 years of operation and further information required by the FSA. The FSA will not issue an authorisation if it appears that the applicant will not fulfil the criterion of 'sound and prudent management'. An applicant for authorisation must show that it has sufficient resources to carry on insurance business.

The application process can be complex and time consuming. The key to a successful and timely application is to submit a first draft application which considers all the issues in the form and content which meets the **Regulator**'s formal requirements. Preliminary meetings at this stage with advisers and the **FSA** can be crucial to resolve any difficult issues. An application will include the submission of a scheme of operations, which covers details of the underwriting, reinsurance arrangements, investment policy and administration (investments should be appropriately diversified and adequately spread with no excessive reliance placed on any particular type of investment).

The authorisation process takes approximately 6-9 months, as the **FSA** is meticulous in its examination of the application.

5.5 The Regulator's Powers of Intervention

5.5.1 Withdrawal of authorisation

An authorised insurance company can underwrite business in the classes in which it is authorised and up to the level of premium that its solvency will allow.

The ultimate power of the **FSA** is to revoke the authorisation to carry on insurance business. In the context of run-off, an authorised company will have its authorisation withdrawn in respect of new business. This means that the company will be able to carry on insurance business insofar as is necessary to run-off its account, but not underwrite new business.

The grounds under which the **FSA** may withdraw authorisation are many and include:

- failure to satisfy an obligation under the Insurance Companies Act 1982 (as amended) or the Financial Services Act 1986;
- failure to satisfy obligations of another EU state that are applicable to the insurance activities of the company in that state;
- failure to fulfil the requirement of sound and prudent management;
- a ground exists that would prevent the **FSA** from authorising the company, if it were not already authorised; or

- the company has ceased to be authorised in a particular class of business at the place where it has its head office.

Withdrawal of authorisation can be for one, several, or all classes that the company was authorised to underwrite.

5.5.2 Other powers

Failure to comply with regulations may prompt the FSA to exercise its powers of intervention.

The powers available to the FSA are wide ranging. They include:

- restrictions on the custody, categories and use of assets and investments;
- submission of financial information on a more regular basis.

General investigations can include the review of the sound and prudent management procedures as well as the application of the fit and proper persons criteria.

The FSA can also take any other action considered necessary to safeguard the interests of policyholders or potential policyholders against the risk that the Insurer may not be able to meet its liabilities or to fulfil the reasonable expectations of its long-term business policyholders

5.6 Insolvency of Insurers[v]

Definition

There are three definitions of insolvency as follows:

1. An insurance company may be technically insolvent when it fails to meet its statutory margins of solvency.
2. It can also be insolvent on a cashflow basis, i.e. when it is unable to meet its obligations as they fall due, even though its assets may exceed its liabilities; or
3. It can be insolvent on a balance sheet basis, when its assets are insufficient to meet its liabilities, having regard to the company's contingent and prospective liabilities. The calculation of assets and

(v) Due to the fact that Insurers/Reinsurers are monitored internally by the management and externally *inter alia* by the rating agencies; the FSA; shareholders; and investment analysts it is very rare that an Insurer or Reinsurer goes from being a live company to becoming insolvent and going into liquidation. However, it is possible and it does occur on occasions, as shown in the recent case of Black Sea and Baltic.

liabilities is not an exact science, but a company that shows an insolvent position on its balance sheet is clearly insolvent.

If the latter test were to be rigorously applied, many companies would find themselves in difficulties as regards their solvency. At all times, the directors of the company must monitor its position and must ensure that the company is not trading while insolvent[vi]. Should a company in run-off become insolvent, the actions of the directors and professional advisors during the period of run-off (and perhaps even before then) will be the subject of scrutiny and questions as to their personal liability may arise.

Size of the market and factors leading to insolvency

According to Best's Special Report into Insolvency (February 1999), 640 US companies have become insolvent since 1969. Research in 1998 highlighted the following reasons for general insurance insolvencies in the USA for 1969 to 1998.[vii]

Factor leading to insolvency	**No. of companies**	**% of total**
Deficient loss reserves (inadequate pricing)	145	34
Rapid growth	86	20
Alleged fraud	44	10
Overstated assets	39	9
Significant change of business	28	7
Reinsurance failure	22	5
Catastrophe losses	36	8
Impaired affiliate	26	6
Total identified	426	100%
Miscellaneous/unidentified	214	
Total insolvencies	**640**	

Table 11 – Factors leading to insolvency.[viii]

(vi) The Insolvency Act 1986 introduced the concept of wrongful trading. This occurs when a director (or a shadow director) at a time when he or she knew or ought to have concluded that their company was likely to be or become insolvent, failed to take every step to prevent further loss to creditors.

(vii) AM Best, Special Report, February 1999, *Insolvency: Will Historic Trends Return?*

(viii) From table 6, we can see that the biggest cause of insolvency is deficient loss

continued overleaf

Powers of the FSA to petition for the winding-up of a company:

The FSA can petition for the winding-up of an insurance company if:

- it is unable to pay its debts (a balance sheet that shows liabilities exceeding assets will be clear evidence of this).;
- it fails to satisfy an obligation under insurance companies legislation;
- it fails to satisfy obligations under various regulations;
- it fails to keep proper accounting records and the FSA is unable to ascertain its financial position;
- if it appears expedient with regard to the public interest.

Others, such as creditors or the company itself, may also seek to wind-up a company. In most cases the application is made on the grounds that the company is "unable to pay its debts".

The first stage of winding-up for insurance companies, is generally the decision to cease underwriting. At some stage thereafter, during the course of the run-off – or at an early stage, when evaluation is made of the assets and liabilities – it becomes apparent that the company does not have sufficient funds to meet its liabilities.

The form of the winding-up

The Insolvency Act 1986 provides a mechanism and rules for the realisation and disposal of assets. These rules were developed for general, non-insurance companies and may become a costly way of realising the assets of a complex insurance concern. Apart from a Scheme of Arrangement, the only procedure available for an insurance company is Compulsory Liquidation under the supervision of the courts. Basically, under the winding-up order, the courts appoint an Official Receiver, who appoints a liquidator to manage the winding-up of the company. The liquidator is a licensed insolvency practitioner, whose job is to realise assets, agree claims and pay dividends to creditors. He calculates the percentage payout of the losses based upon

---

reserves, being 34% of all cases since 1969. This is associated with underpricing where reserves are based on premiums. The second largest cause is rapid growth, being 20% of all insolvencies. In third place is alleged fraud representing 10% of cases. Taken together, these 3 causes account for almost two-thirds (64%) of all insolvencies analysed in the study. However, it should be noted that there is often a variety of causes, rather than just a single. Best's comments that "more often than not insolvency stems from poor management practices."

the deficiency of the total assets in relation to the total liabilities. The liquidator must identify the causes of the insolvency, and also has a duty to investigate the company's affairs with particular reference to the pre-liquidation activities of the company's directors.

As a consequence of the cost of using the mechanism provided under the Insolvency Act 1986 to realise and dispose of assets, most insurance insolvencies go into schemes of arrangement under s.425 of the Companies Act 1985. These schemes are created by agreement by a vote of the creditors and require a majority of 75 % by value. They are tailor-made insolvency arrangements and as such can be designed to avoid much of the cost attendant upon liquidations. They can provide the company with flexibility and the ability to move swiftly towards a final winding-up and distribution to the creditors.

Insurance insolvencies are very complicated and made more so by the contingent nature of many of the liabilities.

5.7 Forthcoming Changes in Legislation

As we go to press the Financial Services and Markets Act 2000 ("FSM") is about to come into effect. This seeks to revolutionise the regulation of financial services in the UK. Under the FSM, the FSA will become a Super Regulator of a wide range of financial services.

Further details and updated information can be found on the FSA's website at: **www.FSA.gov.uk**

5.8 New Rules for Insurance Companies That Have Ceased to Trade

The FSA is in the process of drafting new rules for insurance companies that have ceased to trade. The FSA's immediate intention is to do no more than codify current regulatory practice and procedures for dealing with companies in run-off.

Insurance legislation has been previously drafted without much attention being given to Insurers that have ceased to trade. It contains some provisions concerning liquidation, but very little that deals with run-off. This has not only created difficulties for companies in run-off, but required both the Treasury and the FSA to apply rules and regulations in a way for which they were not originally designed.

Further details and updated information can be found on the Association of Run-off Companies website at: **www.aroc.org.uk**

CHAPTER 6: SHORTCOMINGS OF CURRENT SOLUTIONS

The drive for fairness and equality for all policyholders often leads to a protracted run-off period. The run-off solution (chosen in approximately 90% of cases of discontinued business) does not deliver finality or certainty in the vast majority of cases. It may need additional reinsurances or capital injections over the course of time.

6.1 Categorisation of Shortcomings

We can distinguish between certain categories of problems:

- certain solutions do not extinguish the liabilities but merely transfer the risk to another carrier – for example, the insurance solutions of conventional reinsurance; portfolio transfer, and alternative risk transfer products; and the non-insurance solutions of sale, and statutory transfer of the book of business under Schedule 2C. The financial security of the new risk taker is therefore a consideration, especially for the Regulator who protects the interests of the policyholders.

  This can be compared to solutions that actually extinguish the liabilities e.g. pro-active run-off which encompasses a commutation strategy, and solvent schemes of arrangement;

- the inherent uncertainty in a portfolio regarding ultimate liabilities creates practical barriers to the implementation of certain solutions such as the insurance solutions of conventional reinsurance; portfolio transfer, and alternative risk transfer products; and the non-insurance solutions of sale, and statutory transfer of the book of business under Schedule 2C of the Insurance Companies Act 1982;

- perversely, any solution that financially strengthens a run-off company may significantly hinder commutation negotiations and therefore jeopardise the chances of reaching finality. (This is because Cedants of run-off companies may not be willing to commute with a financially strong company, but prefer to take some money now from a financially impaired company).

Furthermore, the range of problems faced will not be the same for all companies in run-off. Diagram 3 overleaf shows the contrasting problems faced by a company in run-off showing the effects of two factors:

1. The nature of the portfolio – whether the book of business written by the company is largely characterised as being short or long-tail. Short-tail risks are generally those whose claims are normally settled within say 3 – 5 years (examples are property risks). Long-tail risks may last up to 50 years (examples are casualty risks).Whilst most companies have a mix of liabilities, most will emphasise either one or the other;

2. Resources – whether a run-off company has limited or more flexible resources available to it (principally from its parent company). Resources here relate mainly to finances but other resources such as staff and IT are also essential.

Diagram 3:
The contrasting problems faced by entities in run-off

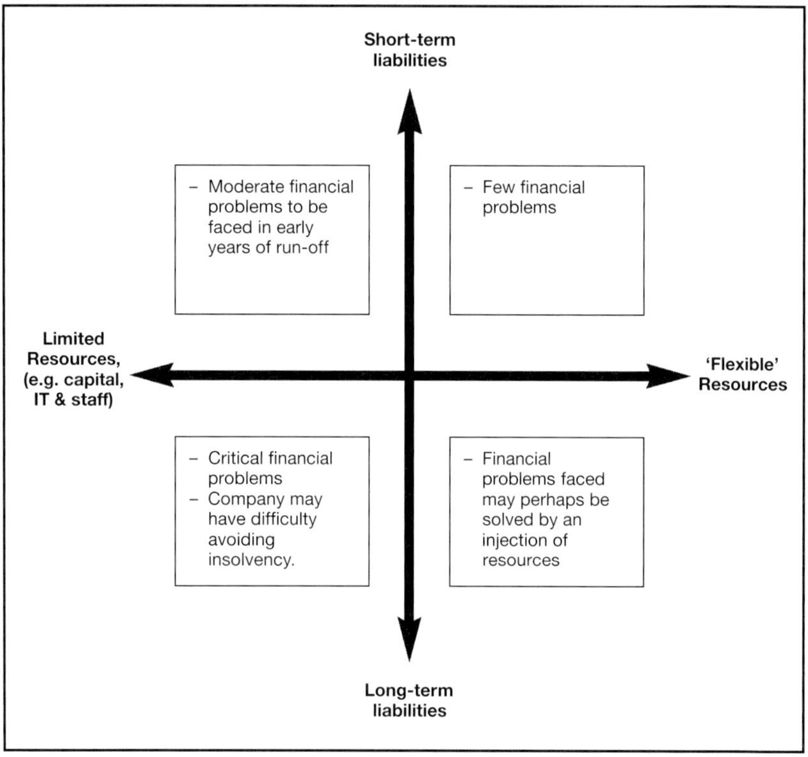

As can be seen from this diagram, there is a distinction to be drawn between companies which have short-tail liabilities and those which have long-tail liabilities:

- at one extreme there are companies which have short-tail liabilities and flexible resources. Such companies have few financial problems;
- at the other are companies which have long-tail liabilities and limited resources. Such companies have critical financial problems.(These companies may have difficulty avoiding insolvency in the longer term).

6.2 Problems Specific to the Run-off Solution

Once a decision to discontinue writing new business has been taken, one of the options is to enter into formal run-off. This is easily the most common option, perhaps taking place in 90% of all cases. At this time no UK registered London Market Company has completed its run-off without a Scheme of Arrangement of some kind. Very few companies have successfully concluded their run-off – i.e. paid all their claims in full, closed their operation, and left a surplus for their shareholders.

Some would argue that run-off could be regarded as an interim step to a scheme or liquidation. This is based upon the fact that most companies which go into run-off in the UK finish by going insolvent. Some run-offs last only a short time such as Charter Re. Others last somewhat longer. North Atlantic took 15 years to move from solvent run-off to insolvency; British & Overseas took 28 years.

The reasons why the run-off option is so popular is perhaps:

1. It allows a longer time to analyse the data and hopefully to commute the biggest relationships so that the valuation of the company's liabilities is more accurate. With increased certainty in ultimate liabilities, there is an increased chance of a Scheme of Arrangement or some other solution gaining the support of the FSA;

2. The status of being in run-off flows easily from its previous status as a live operation – simply close the underwriting department. Initially, there is no legal obligation to make long-term decisions.

The problems with the current approach to run-off can be summarised as follows:

1. **Run-off administration costs are too high.** The administrative burden and the cost of extinguishing liabilities to finality are often enormous and can take a large proportion of the company's assets. In particular, the expense of processing and collecting reinsurance recoveries can be significant (this is particularly the case where the reinsurance programmes are complex and on a large scale, as in the case of Equitas[i]). As claims are paid, funds available for investment are reduced and investment income reduces correspondingly. Run-off costs tend to increase over time due to wage inflation and price inflation, which pushes up both fixed and variable costs. The result of reducing income and increasing costs is that, over time, investment income is insufficient to meet run-off costs. In many cases and especially in the latter years of the run-off, the costs are disproportionate to the size of the company's assets. The assets tend to be dissipated in the administration of the run-off itself.

2. **Adverse claim deterioration** (i.e. liabilities increasing over the lifetime of the run-off). This is especially the case where long-tail liabilities form the majority of the portfolio in run-off. It can be broken down into various problems:

   - *accelerated inward claims reporting* – the natural reaction of a Cedant on hearing that one of its Reinsurers has ceased underwriting is to look closely at its potential claims recovery position. He may take the view, however illogical, that a company in run-off is more likely to become insolvent, and tend to accelerate the reporting of increased and new claims following the review.

   - *inwards claims already reported* increase in value (this is particularly the case where the original reserves are based on limited knowledge and new more detailed knowledge links such things as medical conditions with underlying causes). This is exacerbated by social inflation meaning that acceptable levels of compensation have increased over time and by increased amounts of litigation at the original policy level. Furthermore, new causes of loss are discovered over the lifetime of the run-off resulting in new inwards claims being made. For example, it is possible for a judge in the US to rule for policy coverage where none had been intended by the

(i) Software programmes, however,(such as XLRAS) can help to calculate excess of loss recoveries.

original Underwriters leaving Reinsurers facing numerous unexpected claims.

3. **Adverse reinsurance deterioration** – this is also a combination of various elements:

- claims inflation means that reinsurance protections that were adequate when business was written can be inadequate by the time long-tail claims come to be paid. In certain cases, reinsurance protections may be exhausted;
- reinsurers becoming insolvent and therefore being unable to pay reinsurance claims in full;
- slow reinsurance recovery resulting from a loss of goodwill with Brokers and Reinsurers whilst not deterioration as such, may have the same effect since it will effect the speed of recovery assumptions made when the run-off plan is put together. A lack of reinsurance recoveries due to lack of goodwill can have a devastating effect upon the lifeblood of any run-off i.e. cashflow;
- the reinsurance asset is a non-performing asset from the perspective of the company in run-off in that it generates no income when recoveries are not being made.

4. **There may be issues with data quality.** Liabilities and assets are extremely difficult to value accurately where it is known that the underlying data cannot be relied upon. This is a separate issue from the correct valuation of a company's liabilities arising from the uncertainty in the nature of the liabilities themselves.

   The data held by the run-off company may be of questionable quality (e.g. data is held on computer but cannot be evidenced by physical documentation; or the data held is incomplete with contractual terms unknown or incorrectly recorded on computer. Alternatively, the Broker may hold the majority of the information and is unable or unwilling to provide the details)[ii]. This is a common problem in cases where the contracts relate to reinsurance contracts dating back over a number of years. Whilst files are unlikely to be fully complete, there comes a point when the quality of data will severely affect the reliability that can be placed on any analysis undertaken.

(ii) Particular problems exist where there is inaccurate recording of available reinsurance protections, the Reinsurers on those protections, and the amounts already collected from such Reinsurers.

Although compensating adjustments may be made, a significant data quality issue may, at the extreme, result in the run-off organization's financial report and accounts being qualified by the auditors.

5. **Specific problems with commutations** – There are several separate problems:

   - policyholders are treated unequally through the process of commutation since some gain good deals and others bad deals. The quality of the deal depends, *inter alia*, upon the negotiation skills of the policyholder *vis-à-vis* the run-off company and the quality of data held by each party;
   - an approach of aggressive commutation takes significant time and resource;
   - it may be impractical to commute substantial parts of the portfolio where certain policyholders/reinsurers simply refuse to entertain the idea of commutation;
   - commuting inwards claims without also commuting outwards claims may have an adverse impact on outward reinsurance recoveries since the recoverability of commuted outstanding and IBNR losses is questionable under reinsurance contracts;
   - there is a balance to be found between retaining funds to invest and commuting liabilities to get a discount on the amounts paid. Therefore a strategy of quick commutation may not always be the best alternative for the solvency of the company because of the loss of the interest income which could have been obtained by allowing the liabilities to be paid slowly. It all depends on the discount being offered in the commutation price.

6. **Loss of goodwill** between an entity in run-off and its Reinsurers, policyholders, inward Brokers and outward Brokers often arises upon the adoption of the run-off solution:

   - policyholders. This is because where the art of pro-active/aggressive run-off is practised, run-off companies seek to restrict the payment of inward claims to those, which are strictly due under the terms of the contract. This may compare starkly with its previous claims handling before going into run-off which may have been conducted on a more commercial basis. Where on-going business relations no longer exist, there is less incentive for companies to reach compromises over claim disputes;

- reinsurers. Companies in run-off may also seek to make more active use of their reinsurance protections. In addition some Reinsurers take the view that a reinsurance debt due to a company in run-off is somehow of a lower priority than a reinsurance debt due to a live company;[iii]
- brokers. These may not be prepared to incur avoidable service costs when a client is no longer a source of future business. In short, when a company is no longer contributing to profits it is likely to be low on the list of priorities.

One way in which goodwill is lost is where run-off companies, in an attempt to improve cash flow, have an unofficial policy of slowing down the payment of inward claims. Similarly, run-off companies may decide to withdraw their membership of central settlement systems (i.e. an accounting bureau where accounts are settled between parties via a central clearinghouse under automatic settlement arrangements). This again slows down inward claim payments and results in higher processing costs for the Broker. These are significant problems for policyholders.

Any loss of goodwill and lack of confidence in management to settle claims as quickly and efficiently as possible will inevitably lead to Cedants (who may also act as Reinsurers of the company in run-off as is frequently the case in the reinsurance market) and Brokers retaining funds due to the company on outwards claims. Alternatively, Brokers may process reinsurance collection notes very slowly so causing cashflow problems for the company in run-off. In these cases, run-off companies can (if they have the computer systems and market contacts in place) bypass the Broker and go direct to Reinsurers to collect their reinsurance claims.

As discussed earlier in this book, consolidation of all recoveries through one or a limited number of Brokers on a fee basis, based upon a prompt collection and settlement service, may prove very beneficial and cost effective. However, it should be noted that the outwards Broker has already received one fee for the contract (being the brokerage paid by the company at placement of the reinsurance contract) and to receive a claim collection fee

---

(iii) See the *1998 Kwelm Report and Accounts* wherein Chris Hughes, administrator of the Kwelm group at PricewaterhouseCoopers reports on this phenomenon.

in addition may be viewed as slightly impertinent. The ability of the Brokers to hold run-off companies to ransom in this regard is a serious problem and needs to be addressed by the market.

As a result, *inter alia*, of the loss of goodwill, many inwards and outwards claims are disputed or litigated.

7. **Lack of an appropriate run-off strategy (i.e. once the run-off solution is chosen).** Some businesses lack an appropriate run-off strategy to deal with the consequences of run-off. They fail to appreciate and develop the myriad of skills required, be it technical, actuarial or managerial. Furthermore, they fail to realise that a run-off portfolio can be a source of profit if run according to best practice. It would seem as if some run-offs are managed based on the following maxims:

   - focus upon run-down rather than a dynamic business environment;
   - "do whatever you like except spend money".

   In short, the organisation goes into damage limitation mode, cutting expenses (such as office location, personnel, and IT systems) to a minimum without enough consideration of the effect upon efficiency. The prophecy of bad times ahead becomes almost self-fulfilling. The company isolates itself from the market and in turn is isolated by the market.

   The lack of an appropriate strategy leads in turn to a protracted run-off period and frequently results in an unsatisfactory outcome for all parties concerned – insolvency. There is both a great need and reward for developing a more formalised run-off strategy to deal effectively with the problem of run-off, as it will enable the Insurer/Reinsurer in run-off to face the future with greater certainty. He can take steps to realise specific goals, which often relate to the return of capital to the shareholders, rather than dissipating all the assets in the administration of the run-off itself. In short, control is retained and business efficiency is optimised. The current reluctance to plan for finality in the London Market is based, *inter alia*, upon:

   - the difficulties in assessing a fair deal for policyholders;
   - the third party administrators' vested interest in keeping the run-off going as long as possible to generate fee income where the service contract is based on processing transactions. (This

is a serious problem and needs to be addressed by the market – there needs to be some incentive for the early termination of a company's liabilities).

Winners and losers

In summary, the winners and losers from the current situation in which run-off is conducted are:

- losers – shareholders; policyholders; Brokers;
- winners – third party outsource providers (who administer run-off's on behalf of companies, some badly and some well); Actuaries; Accountants; Reinsurance Consultants; Lawyers; and Insolvency Practitioners.

6.3 Problems specific to the solvent scheme solution

Solvent Schemes of Arrangement (which may be appropriate for many companies in the early years of a run-off before the increased administration costs of the run-off process highlighted above begin to have a serious financial impact on the company) may be:

- too late – many run-off companies eventually become insolvent;
- too expensive – a solvent Scheme of Arrangement requires the services of at least four professionals:

  a. Reinsurance technical consultants to investigate the appropriate reserving and to value the known liabilities and assets.

  b. Actuaries to value the future liabilities.

  c. Accountants to value assets and liabilities on a financial/ balance sheet analysis, and to oversee the scheme.

  d. Lawyers to draft the scheme documents.

- too complex – since each scheme must be tailor-made for the particular company's requirements

Consequently solvent schemes of arrangement are not used enough because run-off companies are deterred from using them.

CHAPTER 7: NEW SOLUTIONS

Only an early exit can significantly reduce administration costs and staunch claim deterioration, releasing as much as US$ 45 billion in shareholder equity trapped in the global run-off market.

A review is needed with the following aims:

- **to reduce the length of time taken to run-off liabilities (the so called 'early exit')- this alone would solve many current problems;**
- **to reduce the cost of run-off in terms of the administrative costs – because investment income is likely to reduce as the run-off progresses (as claims are paid and funds for investment are depleted), then it is essential that administration costs are reduced as well;**
- **to introduce specific insurance insolvency legislation so that the modern practice of utilising a section of the Companies Act not specifically designed for the purpose is no longer necessary;**
- **to learn from the experience of companies currently in run-off and produce a code of best practice.**

The overriding objective should be to preserve the assets of the insurance company for the good of the policyholders and shareholders and to release any remaining capital to shareholders within a predetermined timeframe.

In short, companies must be forced to plan for finality. Decisive action is required.

It is estimated[i] that the run-off costs and net future claims deterioration, to the end of run-off, could amount to US$100 billion and US$ 50 billion respectively. In addition, it is estimated[ii] that US$ 45 billion of shareholder equity could be trapped in the global run-off market. Such equity is not available to generate revenue from new business.

In terms of meeting the overriding objective set out above, the most successful solution used in the marketplace today is perhaps the *solvent* scheme of arrangement. The first was put in place in the

---

(i-ii) PricewaterhouseCoopers – *The managed exits of the future – how to save US$ 50 billion* November 1999.

London market for HIR (UK) Limited in 1998. Solvent schemes and mass commutations are probably the only solutions which bring true finality (outside of a sale of the business, and statutory transfer of the book of business which can be difficult to effect in terms of finding a willing counterparty and the approval of the FSA).

The advantages of an early exit for the run-off were outlined under the pro-active run-off approach, but can be quickly summarised as being:

- it creates certainty – asbestos, pollution, and other health-hazard risks are still subject to material uncertainty as reflected in the recent upsurge in the notifications of asbestos-related claims. Actuaries forecast up to 50 years to conclude casualty reinsurance claims involving toxic tort;
- it reduces run-off administration costs – these costs are material, estimated at 20% of gross liabilities;[iii]
- it reduces interest rate risk – companies in run-off focus on investment income. As claims and run-off administrative costs are paid, funds available for investment are depleted;
- it reduces exposure to claims deterioration – companies prefer to recognise losses today rather than incur continual deterioration over many years in the future;
- it reduces exposure to adverse reinsurance deterioration – in terms of bad debts and exhausted reinsurance cover;
- it allows earlier settlement of creditor's claims than would otherwise be the case;
- for run-off entities that are part of a group of companies, it reduces the time over which capital is tied up in the run-off market and frees management to focus on on-going and new business.

According to recent research, halving the length of run-off could have the effect of halving claim deterioration (in which case a cost saving of US$ 25 billion could be made), and it could perhaps save one-third of the administration costs of run-off (achieving an additional saving of US$ 30 billion). Any exit would also release the trapped equity of US$ 45 billion.

(iii) PricewaterhouseCoopers – *The managed exits of the future – how to save US$ 50 billion* November 1999.

7.1 Project Jupiter

7.1.1 The concept

This is an ambitious market-wide solution to exit discontinued insurance business and release trapped shareholder value championed by PricewaterhouseCoopers in association with Lovells. They regard the insurance run-off industry as suffering from inertia due, *inter alia*, to its mass. Although developed for London market business the solution may be applicable to overseas markets.

In most cases, Project Jupiter provides for the **sale** of the run-off company to a single entity, "Jupiter", (or in the event the company writes on-going business, but has lines of business in run-off, the sale of the run-off portfolio to a dedicated special purpose vehicle controlled by Jupiter). Jupiter will arrange for an outsourcing solution for the combined run-off of its newly acquired subsidiaries before, ultimately, bringing finality to the discontinued business.

7.1.2 The key benefits

The key benefits of this solution are:

- flexibility;
- finality;
- potential to share in value creation;
- economies of scale.

7.1.2.1 Flexibility

The transfers into Jupiter may be outright sales for cash, or for 'equity' in Jupiter or both. The Jupiter outsourcing solution can be utilised without necessarily transferring the risks. Other variations are also possible and can be tailored to the needs of the parties.

Run-off protocols can be developed and agreed with the current owners, to ensure that the vendor is comfortable with the quality of future run-off management. The outsourcing aspect can also provide for a level of continuing involvement in run-off management by the vendor. Alternatively, the vendor can divest complete control of the run-off business.

Reinsurance can be provided to give financial certainty. High-level whole account stop loss reinsurance can effectively cap potential claim deterioration and satisfy the requirements of the FSA. Innovative approaches to funding the reinsurance premiums have been developed by certain Reinsurers.

Each participant would have a different financial position dependent upon the characteristics of the business transferred and the structure adopted.

7.1.2.2 Financial finality

The exit route is tailored to the characteristics of the relevant portfolio, including, for example:

- provision of a bar date for submission of claims,
- actuarial assessment of ultimate liabilities,
- commutation – based upon a net present value discount and appropriate payment arrangements.

Finality also gives an opportunity, when it is appropriate to do so, to achieve an early exit for the run-off.

7.1.2.3 Potential to share in value creation

As outlined above, through Jupiter, vendors may seek sale of their run-off businesses from the outset. If this is the case, the financial outcome for the vendors is of course determined by the sale price.

Alternatively, retaining an interest in Jupiter also allows the vendor to participate in any value created through the benefits of the economies of scale. These include:

- utilising the best people and practices from the existing market;
- investing in the best business processes and IT;
- unwinding inter-entity transactions and collapsing reinsurance spirals;[iv]
- recombining the Underwriters on the policy, to process transactions once in the market efficiently and effectively;
- greater negotiating power, for example in achieving "global" (inwards and outwards) commutations;

(iv) A so-called spiral effect occurs when excess of loss Reinsurers extensively underwrite each other's excess of loss protections. This leads to a transfer of exposures to the same players within the market rather than their dispersal outside the market.

- rationalising infrastructure, for example, transferring back-office functions to a low-cost location.

Jupiter is an attempt to maximise shareholder value by:

- avoiding the risk of adverse claims deterioration;
- minimising reinsurance deterioration, run-off administration costs, and investment earnings volatility.

At the same time, it tries to balance the interests of other stakeholders and removes an unnecessary distraction for management (where the run-off entity is part of a group).

It is likely that the regulator would welcome the concept of a market-wide solution for discontinued business so long as policyholders were no worse off.

7.2 Pooling Outwards Reinsurance Collections

This is a partial solution being considered by a small section of the run-off market. It's attractions lie in it's simplicity and the fact that the entities involved can continue to follow their own independent discontinued business strategy based upon their own particular circumstances.

The Association of Run-off Companies (ARC)[v] based in London, whose membership includes more than 30 companies with portfolios in run-off, is looking to cut costs by pooling outwards reinsurance collections. They are looking to consolidate in order to save costs.

The first planned step is to migrate outwards reinsurance collections form their current Brokers to a new service provider who will deal with several members' collections at one time, perhaps on a principal-to-several-principals basis. This would require a service provider who is willing to agree to guaranteed levels of service.

The essence of the ARC approach is to leave the assets where they lie, centralising only certain processes. This avoids the costs of due diligence which is required when portfolios are sold.

(v) The Association of Run-off Companies was formed in 1998 as a direct result of a desire to exercise more influence over new claims processes in the London Market and to be involved at all consultative stages on all new or proposed developments where the focus was claims-related. It is recognised by the Financial Services Authority ("FSA") and the Association of British Insurers ("ABI")"and is a not for profit organisation run for and by its membership.

7.3 Equitas II Model

7.3.1 The concept

Similar to Jupiter above, this would involve two or more large companies with significant London Market exposures transferring their liabilities to a separate legal entity who would be sufficiently capitalised to ensure the venture's continued solvency until all liabilities were at an end.

On the administrative side, a third party administrator could be appointed to handle operations such as claims, commutations, and investment on a day-to-day basis.

7.3.2 Feasibility

The big advantage that Equitas has over all other solutions is that it can never become insolvent – instead it has a proportionate payment plan which becomes effective in the event that Equitas is unable to meet its claims in full. At this point the link between the old Lloyd's and Equitas would come under scrutiny and although the individual Names would be legally liable for the shortfall, in practice it is likely that Lloyd's would be a target for the shortfall. A. M. Best has built such an eventuality into its rating of Lloyd's. Equitas was granted this dispensation because the individual bankruptcy (and in a very limited number of cases even suicide) of a number of high profile individuals who had entered into contracts on an unlimited liability basis had become a political issue in the UK. Their losses had been caused by an unlikely combination of factors including asbestos-related claims, pollution claims, the Piper Alpha disaster, Hurricane Hugo and the LMX spiral. The dispensation was granted by the DTI but the decision was taken at the very highest level of government that a workable solution had to be found because the huge losses and uncertainty over future liabilities endangered Lloyd's existence. It is unlikely that such dispensation would be granted to a group of shareholders of a limited liability company whose existence is not crucial to the importance of London as a world financial centre as in the case of Lloyd's. The political will would simply not exist. Therefore, the feasibility of the potential insolvency aspect of the Equitas II model is fatally flawed. There is also the issue of how any surplus would be allocated to the various participating parties.

7.3.3 Hypothetical advantages of the Equitas II model:

Notwithstanding the flaws of an Equitas II model, as outlined above, the model of Equitas has so far worked well for Lloyd's. The company's financial strength has actually increased since it took on the run-off of Lloyd's 1992 and prior years of account. However, it is accepted that it is early days in the development of that particular company.[vi] The hypothetical advantages of Equitas II model include the following:

- economies of scale being achieved leading to a reduction in the administration costs of run-off;
- it would be able to receive a higher rate of interest on its investments due to the larger amounts involved;
- Equitas II could develop professionalism in run-off – by focusing on run-off and commanding the resources to attract the best staff. Furthermore, in-house expertise in important areas such as law, IT, and strategy, would be on-hand;
- Equitas II could utilise tried and tested methods and working practices;
- longer planning horizon – the business is seen as a going-concern rather than being in the latter stages of its life. This mental attitude can be critical since the motivation to operate at the most efficient level and to offer a high quality of service is often lost during the latter years of a run-off's existence;
- its huge liabilities would provide it with access to unrivalled claims information and thus it would be in a better position to negotiate with the market;
- the companies for which Equitas II would be responsible would have a single voice. This would be advantageous for its counter-parties who could deal with one party rather than a large number of different companies;
- critical mass – due to its sheer size, Equitas II could be an important voice in the industry and therefore shape the industry to some extent.

(vi) While in the short term Equitas is on track it is important not to lose sight of the inherent uncertainties in Equitas' business, and in particular of its long-tail asbestos, pollution and health hazards related liabilities.

7.4 Fixed Run-off Period

Another approach would be to introduce:

- a fixed run-off period of say, five years (which would allow time for the liabilities to develop to some extent and for the major relationships to be commuted);
- followed by a statutory (solvent) scheme of arrangement . Such a scheme would encompass:
  - statutory estimation of long-tail claims by an obligatory actuarial method. (However, it is accepted that a mature book of business is much easier to accurately estimate on an actuarial basis);
  - acceleration of reinsurance recoverables, related to such claims.

During this five year period other insurance and non-insurance solutions may be used to deal with the liabilities, bearing in mind the disadvantages of each of these solutions as outlined above.

Certain professionals in the run-off market regard fixed run-off as the ideal, but although the advantages are obvious, liquidators and actuaries continue to be concerned that IBNR cannot be accurate enough to adopt this approach.

7.5 Statutory Run-off.

At present, there is no statutory run-off. This is surprising given the large number of insurance and reinsurance entities which have decided to discontinue underwriting, either in whole or in part.

Schemes of Arrangement bring their own difficulties, most notably in terms of delay and costs, as identified by the DTI in December 1994 in its consultative document *'Proposals for Dealing with Insolvent Non-Life Insurance Companies'*. In this document the DTI proposed that a new procedure, statutory run-off, should be created which would adopt all the good features of schemes and liquidations. In a nutshell the DTI proposed that companies, whether solvent or insolvent, should be able to go into statutory run-off.

On application to the Court a licensed insolvency practitioner would be appointed scheme promoter to investigate and, if thought practicable, promote a scheme as an alternative to liquidation. If those proposals were accepted by creditors and subject to approval by both the DTI and the Court, the scheme would become effective under the control of a scheme supervisor, again a licensed insolvency practitioner with a creditors' committee.

The scheme supervisor would have all the powers of investigation and the same remedies against delinquent directors and others as a liquidator. As for his and his committee's powers, duties and responsibilities, these would be set out in rules which would supplement the primary legislation.

This proposal has been superseded by proposals to introduce administration for insurance companies contained in the Financial Services and Markets Act 2000.

7.6 New Form of Scheme of Arrangement

Certain companies are working a new variant of the Scheme of Arrangement whereby companies in run-off agree with policyholders to cap liabilities and make immediate settlement of the net present value of estimated unpaid ultimate liabilities. In addition, Reinsurers are co-opted to participate in the solution.

INDEX